ROMANCE

WITHOUT RESERVATIONS

ROMANCE

WITHOUT RESERVATIONS

great taste

Acknowledgements

Produced by Michael Fagien

Edited by Lori and Michael Fagien

Designed by Buster O'Connor /eye4, inc.

Layout & Production by Lee Seabrook /eye4, inc.

Copy Edited by Candace Nelson

Assistant Edited by Juliet Sink

Recipes are excerpted from Food & Wine Books' *Simply Elegant*
and can be ordered directly by calling 1-800-284-4145
Photography by Ellen Silverman

Special thanks to Barney Cohen and Hillel Kaplan at Valley Entertainment,
Mark Stanich, Judith Hill and David Geller at American Express Publishing,
Heidi Diamond and Amy Rosen at the Food Network and all of the great
restaurants and chefs that have helped us to understand their world.

great taste

Preface

MICHAEL FAGIEN

Like the performing artists who tell us how much they love their work—getting in front of people and sharing their creative sides and passions with an audience—we bring you Great Taste.

While Lori (my partner in so many ways) and I have spent the last two decades applying some of our own passions in the music world—launching music magazines and record labels—not an evening passes in our hectic lives and travel schedules of business lunches and dinner meetings without us seeking out the best restaurants in each city we visit. And whenever we have the chance to cook at home, we love to experiment with great recipes from the chefs and restaurants that we cherish, prepare a relaxing candlelight dinner and top it off with a great CD to add a certain musical ambience. In fact, the food experience has become a passion for us along side music. So when we decided to launch Great Taste, it seemed fairly natural to combine our business and pleasure experiences and create elegant packages of great recipes in a book that comes with great music to complement the experience—music and food done in great taste.

To ensure that our level of understanding the culinary world began to approach that of the music business, we have spent years meeting a lot of well-known and some lesser known master chefs from some of the world's finest dining establishments who helped us to understand and to learn—beyond our sheer enjoyment of this kind of artistry. With the help of our friends at Food & Wine Magazine, we were able to select some of the world's finest recipes and creations from the best in the business. With our immense experience in publishing, we created the Great Taste cookbook that is easy to follow, practical in design and yet highly stylized too! You'll immediately notice its unique and elegant design, yet how easy the book opens on the counter top. And while the music on the CD was carefully produced and selected to accompany and enhance the book, you'll also appreciate how we purposely created its own CD case so that you can store the book with your other cookbooks and the disc in your music-listening area.

We hope that you enjoy our Great Taste cookbooks and CDs as much as we have sharing our own creative sides and passions with you through these culinary and musical selections. We also hope you agree that the name is befitting and done in great taste. Indulge in some of the gourmet selections with friends, play the music in the background while you cook and during the dining experience, and be sure to check out some of our other Great Taste themes.

You can find out more about some of our other creations at www.milor.com.

Enjoy!

Lori and Michael Fagien

Contents

Contents

Hors d'Oeuvres

Belgian Endive Leaves with Herbed Chevre

MAKES ABOUT 30 LEAVES

For an appealing combination, top crisp endive leaves with a mixture of fresh goat cheese, scallion and parsley. The chopped walnuts round out the flavor of the tangy cheese but can be omitted if you're in a rush. Since the saltiness of cheese varies from one producer to the next, you should taste the topping for salt before adding any; you may find that none is needed.

6 ounces mild goat cheese, such as Montrachet, at room temperature

3 tablespoons heavy cream

1 scallion including green top, minced

1 tablespoon minced fresh parsley

⅛ teaspoon salt (if needed)

Large pinch fresh-ground black pepper

2 large heads Belgian endive, leaves separated

¼ cup walnuts, chopped fine (optional)

In a medium bowl, combine the cheese, cream, scallion, parsley, salt, if needed, and pepper. Beat with a wooden spoon until smooth and creamy. Mound or pipe about 1½ teaspoons of the mixture onto each endive leaf. Sprinkle the walnuts, if using, on top.

MAKE IT AHEAD

You can prepare the cheese mixture hours in advance. Top the leaves up to an hour or two ahead. Keep, loosely covered with damp paper towels, in the refrigerator.

Variation

Belgian Endive Leaves with Roquefort and Walnuts

MAKES ABOUT 30 LEAVES

Roquefort replaces the goat cheese, and walnuts are stirred into the creamy filling for this easy alternative.

6 ounces Roquefort or other blue cheese, at room temperature

2 tablespoons heavy cream

¼ cup walnuts, chopped fine

1 tablespoon minced fresh parsley

Large pinch fresh-ground black pepper

2 large heads Belgian endive, leaves separated

In a medium bowl, combine the cheese, cream, walnuts, parsley and pepper. Beat with a wooden spoon until smooth and creamy. Mound about 1½ teaspoons of the mixture onto each endive leaf.

Grilled Scallops with Salsa Verde

SERVES 8

A bowl of zesty, brilliant-green salsa surrounded by grilled scallops makes an attractive dish that's uncommonly delicious. The scallops are great served hot, warm or at room temperature. So you can prepare this hors d'oeuvre ahead or at the last minute, depending on your schedule. Shrimp is a fine alternative to the scallops, and the dipping sauce also works well with raw vegetables.

1	3-inch piece French baguette or bread equivalent, crusts removed
1¼	cups flat-leaf parsley leaves
1	tablespoon capers
3	anchovy fillets
2	tablespoons minced onion
1	clove garlic, minced
2½	teaspoons red-wine vinegar
¾	teaspoon salt
	Fresh-ground black pepper
½	cup plus 2 tablespoons olive oil
¾	pound bay scallops, or sea scallops cut in half horizontally

1. Soak the bread in a bowl of water until the bread is moist throughout, and squeeze to remove as much water as possible. In a blender, puree the bread, parsley, capers, anchovies, onion and garlic with the vinegar, ½ teaspoon of the salt and ¼ teaspoon pepper. With the blender running, add ½ cup of the oil in a thin stream.

2. Light the grill or heat the broiler. Stick a toothpick into each scallop. Brush with the remaining 2 tablespoons oil and sprinkle with ⅛ teaspoon pepper and the remaining ¼ teaspoon salt. Grill or broil the scallops, turning once, until just done, about 3 minutes.

3. Spoon the salsa verde into a small serving bowl set on a platter and arrange the scallops around it. Serve the scallops hot, warm or at room temperature.

MAKE IT AHEAD

The salsa keeps for several days. If you want to serve the scallops at room temperature, make them early, cool, cover and refrigerate. Take them out about thirty minutes before serving so that they're not too cold to have any flavor.

11

12

Shrimp and Guacamole in Mini-Pitas

MAKES 24 MINI-SANDWICHES

Avocado and shrimp are always a great combination. You can be sure everyone will like these charming miniature sandwiches. Choose Hass avocados or another variety from California for the best flavor.

24	small shrimp
2	avocados, preferably Hass
¼	cup plus 1 tablespoon chopped cilantro, plus additional leaves for garnish
2	tablespoons lime juice
1	teaspoon salt
	Pinch fresh-ground black pepper
1	teaspoon olive oil
24	mini-pitas, about 2 inches across

1. In a large pot of boiling, salted water, cook the shrimp until just done, about 2 minutes. Drain and, when the shrimp are cool enough to handle, peel. Cover and refrigerate.

2. In a medium bowl, combine the avocados, ¼ cup of the cilantro, the lime juice, ¾ teaspoon of the salt and the pepper. Mash with a fork until smooth.

3. In a medium bowl, toss the boiled shrimp with the remaining 1 tablespoon cilantro, the oil and the remaining ¼ teaspoon salt.

4. Cut the top third off each mini-pita to make a pocket. Spoon the guacamole into the pita pockets, put a shrimp in each, with the tail peeking out, and garnish with cilantro leaves.

MAKE IT AHEAD

All the components of these pitas can be prepared a day ahead, but they should not be assembled until shortly before serving. Cook and peel the shrimp, cover well and refrigerate. Make the guacamole. Cover it with plastic wrap, pressing the wrap directly on the surface of the guacamole, and refrigerate. If the surface darkens slightly, stir the guacamole just before assembling the pitas.

Tip

Colorful Guacamole

Forget those tricks you've heard about how to keep guacamole green—such as saving the avocado pit and leaving it in the guacamole. Exposure to air makes the flesh of the avocado discolor; so oxygen is what you want to avoid. Covering guacamole with plastic wrap placed directly on the dip's surface keeps it as airtight as possible.

13

14

Mussels on the Half-Shell with Cilantro

MAKES 4 DOZEN MUSSELS

Even though this hors d'oeuvre is made with just a handful of ingredients, it's filled with flavor. Choose small mussels, if you can find them, for a sweeter taste and more elegant look.

4 dozen mussels, scrubbed and debearded

¼ cup olive oil

¼ cup finely chopped cilantro

2 tablespoons minced shallot

½ teaspoon salt

½ teaspoon fresh-ground black pepper

1. Discard any mussels that have broken shells or that do not clamp shut when tapped. Pour 1 inch of water into a large pot. Add the mussels to the pot. Cover, raise the heat to high and bring to a boil. Cook, shaking the pot occasionally, just until the mussels open, about 3 minutes. Remove the open mussels. Continue to cook, uncovering the pot as necessary to remove the mussels as soon as their shells open. Discard any that do not open.

2. Heat the broiler. In a small bowl, combine the oil, cilantro, shallot and salt.

3. Pull off and discard the top shells of the mussels. Arrange the mussels on a baking sheet. Spoon the cilantro mixture over them and sprinkle with the pepper. Broil just until heated through, 1 to 2 minutes.

MAKE IT AHEAD

Cook the mussels a day ahead if you like; either keep them in the shells or pull off the top shells, put the mussels on a baking sheet and cover tightly with plastic wrap before refrigerating. The topping can be stirred together several hours in advance. Then you have only a few minutes of work before serving. If the mussels have been refrigerated, broil an extra minute or so to heat them through.

15

Caviar and Crème Fraîche on Puff-Pastry Squares

MAKES 32 SQUARES

Perfect for special celebrations, these whimsical squares of thin pastry topped with crème fraîche and speckled, à la Jackson Pollock, with caviar, chives and hard-cooked egg are a natural with champagne.

1   5-ounce sheet frozen puff-pastry dough, thawed

1¼ cups crème fraîche

1   ounce osetra or sevruga caviar

2   ounces salmon caviar

1   hard-cooked egg

1   tablespoon chopped fresh chives

1. Heat the oven to 400°. On a floured surface, roll out the puff-pastry dough to a 12-by-16-inch rectangle. Put the pastry on a baking sheet and chill for 30 minutes.

2. Prick the chilled pastry every inch or so with a fork. Bake in the middle of the oven until golden brown on the surface, about 10 minutes. Put a heavy baking sheet on top of the pastry. Reduce the oven temperature to 325° and bake until the pastry is cooked through, about 10 minutes longer. Remove the top baking sheet and let the pastry cool completely on the baking sheet.

3. Spread the crème fraîche in an even layer over the pastry. Scatter the black caviar over half of the pastry and the salmon caviar over the other half. Push the egg through a sieve. Scatter the sieved egg and the chives over all the caviar. Refrigerate just 10 minutes to set the topping.

4. Using a serrated knife, trim the edges and then cut the pastry into 2-inch squares. Serve at once.

MAKE IT AHEAD

Cook the pastry up to eight hours ahead and set it aside at room temperature. With the pastry baked and the toppings ready, these squares are a snap to put together just before serving. Don't assemble ahead of time, or the pastry will get soggy.

17

Tip

Puffless Puff Pastry

Sometimes you want the layered flakiness of puff pastry in a compact form. These squares are a case in point. If you let the pastry rise, it's hard to cut and harder to eat with one hand. A chef's trick that keeps the pastry flat is to put a heavy baking sheet on top of the pastry once it has formed a crust. Use a heavy sheet or a regular light one weighed down with an ovenproof pot.

First Courses

20

Asparagus Soup with Salmon Caviar

SERVES 8

On a warm day, serve this springtime soup cold, rather than hot, for a refreshing first course. The salmon caviar seems to add a touch of luxury even though it's not terribly expensive. If it tastes rather strong, rinse it briefly in cold water.

3 pounds asparagus

9 cups chicken stock or canned, low-sodium chicken broth

2¾ teaspoons salt

4 tablespoons butter

2 leeks, white and light-green parts only, split lengthwise, cut crosswise into thin slices and washed well

⅓ cup basmati or other long-grain rice

2 tablespoons chopped fresh parsley

¼ teaspoon fresh-ground black pepper

1 teaspoon lime or lemon juice

½ cup crème fraîche or sour cream

3 ounces salmon caviar

1. Snap the tough ends off the asparagus and discard them. Cut the tips into two or three slices. Cut the stems into 1-inch pieces. Bring the stock to a boil with 1 teaspoon of the salt. Add the asparagus tips and cook until just done, about 5 minutes. Remove with a slotted spoon or strainer and rinse with cold water. Drain thoroughly and set aside. Reserve the stock.

2. In a large pot, melt the butter over moderately low heat. Add the leeks. Cook, stirring occasionally, until soft, about 5 minutes. Add the reserved stock and the rice. Bring to a simmer and cook, partially covered, until the rice is almost tender, about 20 minutes. Add the asparagus stems and the remaining 1¾ teaspoons salt and cook until just done, about 5 minutes.

3. In a blender, puree the soup with the parsley. Strain the soup back into the pot, pressing the vegetable puree through the sieve with a spoon or ladle.

4. Add the asparagus tips and reheat. Stir in the pepper and lime juice and ladle into individual bowls. Top each serving with a dollop of crème fraîche and some of the salmon caviar.

—Katherine Alford

MAKE IT AHEAD

Complete the soup through step three a day or two before serving. Store the asparagus tips separately so that they don't loose their bright-green color. Reheat and finish the soup shortly before serving.

Wine Recommendation

Asparagus is a famously tough wine match, but a concentrated, well-balanced Alsatian Riesling or pinot blanc will pull it off with style.

21

Green-Bean Salad with Shiitake Mushrooms

SERVES 8

This tasty salad makes a tempting, light first course—just the thing to serve before a substantial main dish.

1½	pounds haricots verts or standard green beans
1	tablespoon olive oil
⅓	pound shiitake mushrooms, stems removed and caps sliced
½	teaspoon chopped fresh thyme, or ⅛ teaspoon dried
1	shallot, minced
¼	cup Classic Vinaigrette, next page
½	teaspoon salt
8	radicchio leaves

MAKE IT AHEAD

Sauté the mushrooms and boil the beans a day or two in advance, if you like. Store them separately in the refrigerator and let them come to room temperature before serving. Don't dress the salad until shortly before serving or the beans will lose their bright-green color.

Wine Recommendation

Look for an herbal-inflected New World sauvignon/fumé blanc or a sémillon with a note of fruitiness.

1. In a large pot of boiling, salted water, cook the beans until tender, about 10 minutes. Drain, rinse with cold water and drain thoroughly. Pat dry with paper towels

2. In a large frying pan, heat the oil over moderate heat. Add the mushrooms and thyme and cook, stirring occasionally, until the mushrooms are brown, about 5 minutes. Add the shallot and cook, stirring, until soft, about 2 minutes longer.

3. In a large bowl, toss the green beans, mushrooms, vinaigrette and salt. Put one radicchio leaf on each of eight plates and arrange the salad in the leaves.

—*Stephanie Lyness*

22

Classic Vinaigrette

MAKES ABOUT ½ CUP

A vinaigrette is the classic French combination of vinegar, oil, salt and pepper. Mustard is often added, and lemon or lime juice can replace the vinegar. We suggest two variations, but feel free to experiment further. Try raspberry, tarragon or balsamic vinegar. A spoonful of walnut or hazelnut oil adds a surprising amount of flavor, and chopped fresh herbs, shallot or garlic is a pleasant addition. Olive oil is hardly traditional (French chefs, except those in Provence, find the flavor too strong for greens), but by all means use it for all or part of the oil, if you like.

2 tablespoons red-wine vinegar

½ teaspoon Dijon mustard

½ teaspoon salt

⅛ teaspoon fresh-ground black pepper

⅓ cup cooking oil, such as peanut, corn or safflower

In a small bowl, whisk together the vinegar, mustard, salt and pepper. Add the oil slowly, whisking.

MAKE IT AHEAD

A vinaigrette will last indefinitely in the refrigerator; so it's convenient to make extra. Store any leftover dressing in a glass jar with a tight lid so that you can shake the vinaigrette to re-emulsify it. Don't add fresh herbs, shallot, scallion or garlic more than a day ahead, or the herbs will lose their vibrant color and the other flavorings will taste stale.

Variation

Sherry-Scallion Vinaigrette

Sherry vinegar has a strong flavor; you don't need much. Make as at left with these ingredients and add the scallion at the end.

2 teaspoons sherry vinegar

½ teaspoon salt

⅛ teaspoon fresh-ground black pepper

⅓ cup cooking oil

2 teaspoons minced scallion

Variation

Lemon-Pepper Vinaigrette

Make as at left with these ingredients.

2 tablespoons lemon juice

½ teaspoon salt

¾ teaspoon fresh-ground black pepper

⅓ cup olive oil

23

24

Spaghetti with Parmesan and Mixed Spicy Greens

SERVES 8

Mustard greens, broccoli rabe and escarole, all intensely flavorful, add real punch to this simple pasta. Play around with the proportions of the different greens to suit your taste. Or try other sturdy, robust leaves such as dandelion, collard or kale.

½	cup pine nuts
⅓	cup olive oil
6	cloves garlic, minced
¾	teaspoon dried red-pepper flakes
¾	pound mixed greens, such as mustard greens, broccoli rabe and/or escarole, tough stems removed and leaves cut into 1½-inch pieces (about 3½ quarts)
¾	teaspoon salt
2	cups chicken stock or canned, low-sodium chicken broth
1	pound spaghetti
1½	cups grated Parmesan cheese, plus more for serving

1. In a small frying pan, toast the pine nuts over moderately low heat, stirring frequently, until the nuts are golden brown, about 4 minutes. Or toast in a 350° oven for 6 minutes.

2. In a large pot, heat the oil over moderately low heat. Add the garlic and red-pepper flakes and cook until the garlic is soft but not brown, about 1 minute. Increase the heat to moderately high, add the greens and salt and cook, stirring, until the greens wilt, 1 to 2 minutes. Add the stock, bring to a simmer and cook 5 minutes longer.

3. In a large pot of boiling, salted water, cook the spaghetti until just done, about 12 minutes. Drain the pasta. Toss with the mixed greens and stock. Add the Parmesan and pine nuts, toss again and serve.

—*Katherine Alford*

MAKE IT AHEAD

Toast the pine nuts days in advance, if you like. You can also clean and sauté the greens well ahead, but don't simmer them in the stock until an hour or two before serving.

25

Wine Recommendation

Try a fruity red with mild tannin such as a Chinon or Bourgueil, cabernet franc–based wines from the Loire. A young Chianti would be delicious as well.

Wild-Mushroom Risotto

SERVES 8

Risotto, made by a uniquely Italian method for cooking rice, is a sophisticated first course for any dinner party. Frequent stirring is required, but you will be rewarded with a creamy dish your guests will truly savor. The rich, earthy flavor of the fresh mushrooms is intensified by dried porcini.

½　ounce dried porcini mushrooms

1　cup boiling water

7 to 8　cups chicken stock or canned, low-sodium chicken broth

1　pound mixed wild mushrooms, such as shiitake, cremini and portobello

4　tablespoons olive oil

3　cloves garlic, minced

3　teaspoons salt

2　shallots, minced

3　cups arborio rice, rinsed

1　cup dry white wine

¾　cup grated Parmesan cheese

5　tablespoons butter, at room temperature

2　tablespoons chopped fresh sage, or 2 teaspoons dried

¼　teaspoon fresh-ground black pepper

1. Put the dried mushrooms in a small bowl and pour the boiling water over them. Soak until softened, about 20 minutes. Remove the mushrooms and strain their liquid into a large pot through a sieve lined with a paper towel. Rinse the mushrooms well to remove any remaining grit and chop them. Add the stock to the mushroom soaking liquid and bring to a simmer.

2. If using shiitakes or portobellos, remove the stems. Slice all the fresh mushrooms. In another large pot, heat 2 tablespoons of the oil over moderate heat. Add the chopped porcini and the sliced fresh mushrooms and cook, stirring occasionally, until brown, about 5 minutes. Add the garlic and ½ teaspoon of the salt and cook, stirring, until the garlic is fragrant, about 30 seconds. Put the mushrooms in a bowl.

3. Heat the remaining 2 tablespoons oil in the pot over moderately low heat. Add the shallots. Cook, stirring occasionally, until translucent, about 3 minutes. Add the rice. Stir until the rice begins to turn opaque, about 2 minutes. Add the wine and the remaining 2½ teaspoons salt and cook, stirring constantly, until all the wine has been absorbed.

4. Add about 1 cup of the simmering stock and cook, stirring constantly, until the stock has been completely absorbed. The rice and stock should bubble gently; adjust the heat as needed. Continue cooking the rice, adding the stock 1 cup at a time, allowing the rice to completely absorb the stock before adding the next cup. Cook the rice in this way until tender, about 30 minutes in all. The stock should be thickened by the starch from the rice. You may not need to

use all of the liquid. Stir in the mushrooms, cheese, butter, sage and pepper
and serve.

—*Stephanie Lyness*

MAKE IT AHEAD

Traditionally, risotto is cooked at the
last minute. However, most of the
process can be done ahead of time.
Even the finest Italian restaurants will
admit to using this trick. Just cook
the rice until it is almost done and set
it and the few remaining cups of
stock aside. Five to ten minutes before
you serve, reheat the stock and pro-
ceed with the recipe. You'll enjoy that
famous creamy texture without the
last-minute fuss.

Tip

It's not likely you'll have any leftover
risotto, but in case you do, here is a
delicious way to enjoy it all over again.
Simply form the cool risotto into
small pancakes and dip into lightly
beaten egg, then into fresh or dry
bread crumbs. Cook the risotto cakes
in butter and oil over moderate heat
until completely warmed through and
golden brown on the outside, ten to
fifteen minutes.

Wine Recommendation

This is a very wine-versatile dish. Since
it's cooked with white wine, you may
want to serve the same or a related
wine, but a pinot noir or young
Chianti would be gorgeous as well.

Variation

Classic
Cheese Risotto

27

This traditional recipe is still the
favorite of many risotto lovers. The
subtle but delicious flavor makes it a
memorable first course. Omit the porcini and boiling water, the fresh mushrooms, shallots, garlic and sage. Bring
9 cups stock to a simmer. Chop 1
onion fine. In a large pot, heat 2 tablespoons olive oil over moderately low
heat. Add the onion and cook, stirring
occasionally, until translucent. Add the
rice and cook the risotto as directed,
using 2½ teaspoons salt. Stir in 1 cup
grated Parmesan cheese with the butter and the pepper.

28

Caribbean Shrimp with Chile Aioli and Mango-Papaya Salad

SERVES 8

Jumbo grilled shrimp are matched with a sweet and savory salad of mangos and papaya. A quick aioli flavored with ancho chile complements the two.

¼ cup olive oil

4 tablespoons lime juice (from about 2 limes)

4 tablespoons light rum

1 clove garlic, chopped

2 small dried red chile peppers

2 teaspoons sugar

1 teaspoon salt

¾ teaspoon fresh-ground black pepper

24 jumbo shrimp, shelled

3 mangos, peeled and cut into ½-inch dice (see "Cutting Mangos," next page)

1 papaya, peeled, seeded and cut into ½-inch dice

½ red bell pepper, cut into ¼-inch dice

¼ cup chopped red onion

1 large jalapeño pepper, seeded and minced

2 tablespoons chopped cilantro

Ancho-Chile Aioli, next page

1. In a large, shallow glass dish, combine the oil with 2 tablespoons of the lime juice, 2 tablespoons of the rum, the garlic, dried red chiles, 1 teaspoon of the sugar, ½ teaspoon of the salt and ½ teaspoon of the black pepper. Add the shrimp and toss to coat. Cover with plastic wrap and marinate in the refrigerator 2 to 3 hours.

2. Light the grill or heat the broiler. Remove the shrimp from the marinade and cook on both sides until done, about 2 minutes per side. Cool and refrigerate until ready to serve.

3. Reserve ¼ cup of the mango for the chile aioli. In a large glass or stainless-steel bowl, combine the remaining mango, the papaya, bell pepper, onion, jalapeño, cilantro and the remaining 2 tablespoons lime juice, 2 tablespoons rum, 1 teaspoon sugar, ½ teaspoon salt and ¼ teaspoon black pepper. Chill until ready to serve.

4. To serve, arrange the shrimp, mango papaya salad and aioli on individual plates.

—*Grace Parisi*

MAKE IT AHEAD

There are three components in this dish, and each can be prepared well in advance. You can make the chile aioli and the mango papaya salad a day ahead. Keep them in the refrigerator. The shrimp can be marinated and grilled several hours before serving them so that once guests arrive, you'll need only to arrange the plates.

Wine Recommendation

A mildly sweet rosé would match both the flavors and the whimsical presentation of the dish. A chilly beer would taste good, too.

29

Notes

Cutting Mangos

There's a trick to removing the flesh from a mango. Stand the unpeeled mango on end and, using a sharp knife, slice down through the skin and flesh, as close as possible to the pit, to remove the flesh in one piece. Repeat on the other side. With the two pieces skin-side down, score the flesh into cubes, taking care not to cut through the skin. Turn the skin "inside out" and slice off the cubes of fruit.

Ancho-Chile Aioli

MAKES ABOUT ¾ CUP

1 dried ancho chile

½ cup boiling water

¼ cup reserved chopped mango (from the mango-papaya salad, previous page)

1 small clove garlic, chopped

½ cup mayonnaise

½ teaspoon lime juice

Pinch salt

1. Put the ancho chile in a small bowl and pour the boiling water over it. Let soak until softened, about 20 minutes. Stem and seed the chile. Scrape the inside of the chile with a small knife to get the pulp.

2. In a food processor or blender, puree the ancho-chile pulp, the reserved mango and the garlic with the mayonnaise, lime juice and salt.

30

Grilled Quail with Cucumber Relish

SERVES 8

Guests are always pleased when offered these luxurious little birds. Here the quail are marinated, grilled and then matched with a crisp cucumber relish. You can add a small mound of dressed mixed salad greens to the plate, if you like.

8 tablespoons lemon juice (from about 2 lemons)

6 tablespoons olive oil

2 teaspoons chopped fresh rosemary, or ¾ teaspoon dried

2 cloves garlic, minced

1½ teaspoons salt

1¼ teaspoons fresh-ground black pepper

8 quail

2 cucumbers, peeled, seeded and cut into ¼-inch dice

2 scallions including green tops, minced

2 tablespoons chopped flat-leaf parsley

1. In a large bowl, combine 6 tablespoons of the lemon juice, 4 tablespoons of the oil, the rosemary, garlic, 1 teaspoon of the salt and 1 teaspoon of the pepper. Add the quail and rub them inside and out with this marinade. Cover and refrigerate for at least 1 hour.

2. In a large bowl, whisk the remaining 2 tablespoons lemon juice, 2 tablespoons oil, ½ teaspoon salt and ¼ teaspoon pepper. Add the cucumbers, scallions and parsley and toss. Cover and refrigerate until ready to serve.

3. Light the grill or heat the broiler. Grill or broil the quail on both sides until just done, about 5 minutes in all. The quail should still be slightly pink inside. Pile the cucumber relish on salad plates and set the quail alongside. Serve while the quail are still hot from the grill and the relish is cold and crisp.

MAKE IT AHEAD

Small birds such as quail should be finished at the very last minute, but they can be prepared and put in the marinade up to three hours before cooking. The cucumber relish, too, can be made a few hours ahead, but don't add the salt until shortly before serving, or it may draw out some of the moisture in the cucumber and make the relish limp and watery.

Wine Recommendation

The quail will accommodate a wide variety of light-to-medium-bodied wines, including such whites as chardonnay and sauvignon blanc, and reds such as Beaujolais or pinot noir.

31

Crab Cakes with Chile Rémoulade

SERVES 8

It seems crab cakes will never go out of style. In this recipe, a minimum of other ingredients is added so that the sweet crab flavor comes through clearly.

1½ pounds lump crab meat, picked free of shell

1¼ cups dry bread crumbs

4½ tablespoons mayonnaise

1½ tablespoons Dijon mustard

¾ teaspoon Tabasco sauce

1¼ teaspoons salt

    Pinch fresh-ground black pepper

¾ cup flour

2 eggs, beaten to mix

    Cooking oil, for frying

    Chile Rémoulade, next page

1. In a medium bowl, combine the crab, ¼ cup of the bread crumbs, the mayonnaise, mustard, Tabasco sauce, salt and pepper. Shape the mixture into sixteen ¾-inch-thick cakes, about ¼ cup each.

2. Dust the cakes with the flour and pat off the excess. Dip each cake into the eggs and then into the remaining bread crumbs.

3. In a large nonstick frying pan, heat about ½ inch of oil over moderate heat. When the oil is hot, add some of the crab cakes and fry until golden brown and crisp, 2 to 3 minutes. Turn the cakes and fry them until golden brown on the other side, about 2 minutes longer. Drain on paper towels. Repeat until all the crab cakes are fried. Serve with the Chile Rémoulade.

—*Grace Parisi*

MAKE IT AHEAD

You can shape the crab mixture into cakes a day in advance, and you can coat them a couple of hours before frying. Crisp crab cakes are really best served shortly after they are cooked, but you can make them a day ahead, if you need to. Just before serving, put the fried cakes on a baking sheet and reheat in a 400° oven. The rémoulade will keep for days, covered and refrigerated.

Wine Recommendation

This is a classic match for either a chardonnay or a Riesling.

Tip

Bread Crumbs

Store-bought dry bread crumbs work perfectly for crab cakes; so there's no need to make them yourself. If, however, you have stale bread around, making crumbs is a great way to use it up. Leave slices out at room temperature for about 3 hours. Or dry them in a 300° oven for 15 minutes, turning once. Pulverize in a food processor or blender.

32

Accompaniment

Chile Rémoulade

MAKES ABOUT 1 CUP

2 dried or canned chipotle chiles

½ cup boiling water

1 cup mayonnaise

2 teaspoons Dijon mustard

2 teaspoons lime or lemon juice

⅛ teaspoon salt

1. Put the dried chiles, if using, in a small bowl, cover with the boiling water and let soak 20 minutes. Stem and seed the chiles. Scrape the inside of each chile with a small knife to get the pulp. Or remove the seeds from canned chiles.

2. Put the chiles in a small bowl and stir in the mayonnaise, mustard, lime juice and salt.

Information

Chipotle Chiles

Chipotle, a chile widely used in Mexican and Southwestern cooking, is from an Indian word meaning "smoked chile." The name refers to any smoked chile, though smoked *chile gordo*, a fat, fleshy jalapeño that's been allowed to ripen to a dark red, is the most common. The dried peppers are available in many specialty-food stores and increasingly in supermarkets. Dried, brown and shriveled, this less-than-luscious-looking pepper actually has a delicious, smoky flavor and subtle heat that are great additions to soups, salsas and sauces such as the rémoulade at left. Chipotles are also sold canned in adobo sauce.

33

Gravlax with Grainy-Mustard Sauce

SERVES 8

You're sure to impress your guests with home-cured salmon, and they'll never imagine how easy this Swedish favorite is to prepare.

3 pounds center-cut salmon fillet, with skin intact and pinbones removed

2 tablespoons peppercorns

⅓ cup coarse salt

¼ cup sugar

1 large bunch dill

2 tablespoons vodka

¼ cup grainy mustard

¼ cup sour cream

1. Cut the salmon crosswise into two equal pieces. Crush the peppercorns with a rolling pin or in a mortar with a pestle. Combine the peppercorns, salt and sugar.

2. Lay the salmon on a work surface, skin-side down, and press the salt mixture onto the fish. Put a third of the dill on the bottom of a shallow glass baking dish. Put a piece of the salmon, skin-side down, on the dill. Top with another third of the dill and sprinkle with the vodka. Top with the second piece of salmon, skin-side up, and the remaining dill. Cover with plastic. Set a plate on the salmon and a weight on the plate (two 28-ounce cans work well). Leave the salmon to cure in the refrigerator for at least 24 hours and up to 3 days. Turn the fish two or three times while it cures and baste it occasionally with the juices.

3. In a small bowl, combine the mustard and sour cream. Discard the dill and pat the fish dry with paper towels. Cut the fish into the thinnest possible diagonal slices. Serve with rye bread and the mustard sauce.

MAKE IT AHEAD

Gravlax must be prepared one to three days in advance. And once cured it will keep for several additional days. You can also slice it early on the day you plan to serve it.

35

Wine Recommendation

A fine-quality Gewürztraminer will taste like an orchard full of exotic fruit with this combination.

Warm Portobello and Basil Salad

SERVES 8

Portobello mushrooms are so big and meaty that they're often compared to steak. And, like steak, they're wonderful grilled or broiled.

3 pounds portobello mushrooms, stems removed

8 tablespoons olive oil

4 cloves garlic, minced

3 tablespoons chopped fresh basil

1½ teaspoons salt

⅛ teaspoon fresh-ground black pepper

6 ounces mixed salad greens (about 9 cups)

1. Light the grill or heat the broiler. Put the mushrooms in a large bowl, drizzle with 6 tablespoons of the oil, add the garlic and toss. Grill or broil about 5 inches from the heat, turning three or four times, until softened and lightly browned, 8 to 10 minutes. Return the mushrooms to the bowl. Add the basil, salt and pepper and toss gently.

2. Mound the salad greens on individual plates. Slice the mushrooms, return them to the bowl and toss them with the remaining 2 tablespoons oil. Arrange on top of the greens.

MAKE IT AHEAD

You can toss the mushrooms with the oil and garlic several hours in advance and set aside at room temperature. Grill them and assemble the salad shortly before serving.

Wine Recommendation

Go red on this one. A fruity, spicy dolcetto from Piemonte or a Côtes du Rhône captures the meaty savor.

36

Notes

Main Courses

40

Salmon in Scallion Broth

SERVES 8

A distinctively green scallion broth is a lovely and delicious background for salmon fillets. Be sure not to overcook the fish, or it will be dry and bland. Take it from the oven when the interior is still slightly undercooked; by the time it gets to the table it will be done perfectly.

1 tablespoon butter

12 scallions including green tops, chopped

1 cup chicken stock or canned, low-sodium chicken broth

1 cup water

1 teaspoon salt

¼ teaspoon fresh-ground black pepper

3 pounds skinless salmon fillets, cut into 8 pieces

1. Heat the oven to 450°. In a medium pot, melt the butter over moderately low heat. Add the scallions and cook, stirring occasionally, until wilted, about 3 minutes. Add the stock, water and ½ teaspoon of the salt. Raise the heat and bring to a boil. Reduce the heat and simmer 2 minutes.

2. With a slotted spoon, transfer the scallions to a blender and puree with a few tablespoons of the cooking liquid. Add the remaining liquid and blend until very smooth, about 2 minutes. Return the scallion broth to the pot and add the pepper.

3. Oil a baking sheet. Put the salmon on the baking sheet and sprinkle with the remaining ½ teaspoon salt. Cook in the upper third of the oven until just barely done (it should still be translucent in the center), 5 to 8 minutes. Meanwhile, bring the scallion broth just to a boil. Transfer the salmon to soup plates and pour the broth around the fish.

MAKE IT AHEAD

The scallion broth can be made a day ahead and reheated. You can have the salmon all ready to go and just pop it in the oven five to ten minutes before you want to serve dinner.

Wine Recommendation

The buttery quality and lemony flavor of a California chardonnay or French white Burgundy such as a Meursault highlights the mild sweet-and-salty contrast of this salmon dish.

41

Black-Pepper Seared Tuna with Corn Couscous

SERVES 8

Thick tuna steaks with a crisp, peppery crust and juicy, rare center are luscious-looking when sliced and served encircling a mound of Corn Couscous. We love the contrast of the black pepper with the sweetness of the corn.

3 pounds tuna steaks, about 2 inches thick, cut into 3½-inch pieces

1 tablespoon cooking oil

1 tablespoon fresh-ground black pepper

½ teaspoon salt

Corn Couscous, page 64

1. Light the grill or heat a heavy frying pan until very hot. Brush all sides of the tuna steaks with the oil and sprinkle with the pepper and salt.

2. Sear the tuna on all 4 sides, 1½ minutes per side. Let sit, loosely covered with foil, for 3 minutes. The fish will be rare.

3. To serve, cut the tuna into ¼-inch slices. Put a small mound of the Corn Couscous on each plate, or mound it all on a platter, and arrange the tuna slices, overlapping, around the couscous.

Wine Recommendation

The meaty flavor of the tuna and the spice of the black pepper are a casting call for a medium-bodied red with a contrasting fruitiness. Look for a California pinot noir, a French Chinon or even a merlot.

MAKE IT AHEAD

Here's a dish that's as delicious served at room temperature as it is hot. You can cook the tuna and let it sit at room temperature, covered, for up to two hours before serving. At the last minute, slice it and serve with room-temperature couscous.

Alternative

Don't Like Rare Tuna?

Rare tuna is all the rage these days, but if you prefer it more done, simply buy thinner tuna steaks. If the steaks are one-and-a-half inches thick, the tuna will be medium when cooked the time specified in this recipe. Well-done steaks are sure to be dry.

42

Broiled Swordfish Steaks with Pineapple-and-Chile Salsa

SERVES 8

Broiling is the easiest way to prepare firm, juicy swordfish. Pineapple salsa with ancho chiles makes a refreshing and colorful accompaniment.

3 pounds swordfish steaks (about 1 inch thick)

2 tablespoons cooking oil

½ teaspoon salt

¼ teaspoon fresh-ground black pepper

1 tablespoon butter

Pineapple-and-Chile Salsa

1. Heat the broiler. Brush both sides of the swordfish steaks with the oil and sprinkle with the salt and pepper. Put the swordfish on a baking sheet and dot with the butter.

2. Broil 4 inches from the heat for 2½ minutes. Turn and broil the other side until the fish is just done, about 3 minutes longer. Serve accompanied with the Pineapple-and-Chile Salsa.

MAKE IT AHEAD

The salsa can be made early on the day of the dinner and refrigerated. You can also oil, salt and pepper the fish, cover it well and refrigerate. That leaves just about five minutes of cooking time before you serve. Either bring the fish to room temperature before broiling or add an extra minute of cooking time.

Wine Recommendation

The fruitiness and mild tannin of a *cru* Beaujolais or Beaujolais-Villages, served lightly chilled, will embrace the contrasting flavors of this dish.

Accompaniment

Pineapple-and-Chile Salsa

MAKES 2 CUPS

2 dried ancho chiles

1 cup boiling water

½ pineapple, cut into ¼-inch dice

½ red bell pepper, cut into ¼-inch dice

1 small red onion, cut into ¼-inch dice

¼ cup chopped cilantro

¼ cup orange juice

2 tablespoons lime juice

¼ teaspoon ground cumin

¼ teaspoon salt

Pinch fresh-ground black pepper

1. Put the chiles in a bowl and pour the boiling water over them. Let soak until softened, about 20 minutes. Drain, stem and seed the chiles. Press them through a sieve into a medium glass or stainless-steel bowl.

2. Add the remaining ingredients and stir to combine.

43

Poached Halibut with Cilantro-Lime Mayonnaise

SERVES 8

Halibut served at room temperature is a perfect alternative to the ubiquitous poached salmon. The steaks are easy to divide into serving pieces because of a large central bone, and you can poach them in a large, wide pot or deep, wide frying pan if you don't have a fish poacher.

3 quarts water

3 onions, sliced

3 ribs celery, cut into thirds

2 tablespoons white vinegar

1 bay leaf

8 peppercorns

1½ teaspoons salt

3 pounds halibut steaks, 1½ inches thick

Cilantro-Lime Mayonnaise

1. In a fish poacher or large pot, combine the water, onions, celery, vinegar, bay leaf, peppercorns and salt. Bring to a boil over moderately high heat. Reduce the heat. Simmer, partially covered, for 30 minutes.

2. Add the fish in one layer and bring almost back to a simmer. Let poach, uncovered, until the fish is just done, about 5 minutes. Gently remove the fish and let cool to room temperature. Serve with the Cilantro-Lime Mayonnaise.

Wine Recommendation

A California or Australian sauvignon blanc will complement the creaminess of the mayonnaise and pick up the herb flavor of the cilantro.

MAKE IT AHEAD

This is a great dish to prepare in advance since the fish is served cooled. You can poach the halibut and let it sit at room temperature, covered, for up to two hours before serving. Or you can poach the fish earlier in the day, cool, cover and refrigerate. Remove the halibut from the refrigerator about thirty minutes before you're ready to serve it. The Cilantro-Lime Mayonnaise can be made hours ahead.

45

Accompaniment

Cilantro-Lime Mayonnaise

MAKES 2 CUPS

2½ cups lightly packed cilantro leaves

2 eggs

1½ cups plus 2 tablespoons olive oil

2 tablespoons lime juice

2 tablespoons water

1 teaspoon salt

⅛ teaspoon fresh-ground black pepper

1. In a food processor or blender, puree the cilantro with the eggs.

2. With the machine running, add the oil in a thin stream. Add the lime juice, water, salt and pepper and whir to mix.

Boiled Lobster with Ginger Butter

SERVES 8

Wonderful as lobsters taste served with plain melted butter, they're even better when you flavor the butter with grated ginger, lemon juice and fresh herbs.

8 lobsters (about 1½ pounds each)

1 pound butter

2 tablespoons plus 2 teaspoons grated fresh ginger

2 tablespoons lemon juice

¼ cup chopped flat-leaf parsley

¼ cup chopped cilantro

1 teaspoon salt

¼ teaspoon fresh-ground black pepper

1. In two large pots of boiling, salted water, cook the lobsters until just done, about 10 minutes after the water returns to a boil.

2. Meanwhile, melt the butter over moderate heat in a medium pot. Remove the pot from the heat and add the remaining ingredients. Serve the lobsters with the ginger butter.

MAKE IT AHEAD

Though this dish requires very little preparation, don't forget how long big pots of water take to come to a boil. Put them on well before you intend to cook the lobsters. You can prepare the ginger and herbs several hours in advance. Cover and set aside. Squeeze the lemon juice, too, and season it with the salt and pepper. At serving time, simply melt the butter and add the prepared ingredients.

Wine Recommendation

The balanced sweetness and acidity of a richer-style Riesling from Alsace or Germany (look for a wine of kabinett or spätlese quality) is a lovely match for the sweetness of the lobster and the pungency of the grated ginger.

46

Polenta-Stuffed Cornish Hens

SERVES 8

Cornish hens are split in half and roasted, each atop a mound of rosemary-and-garlic-flavored polenta.

6 tablespoons olive oil

2 cloves garlic, crushed

1 teaspoon chopped fresh rosemary, or ½ teaspoon dried

3 cups water

1 teaspoon salt

1 cup coarse or medium cornmeal

¼ teaspoon fresh-ground black pepper

4 Cornish hens (about 1¼ pounds each), halved

1. In a small saucepan, heat the oil, garlic and rosemary over moderate heat and cook until the garlic is soft but not brown, about 1 minute. Set aside.

2. In a medium saucepan, bring the water and ¾ teaspoon of the salt to a boil. Add the cornmeal in a slow stream, whisking constantly. Reduce the heat to moderate and simmer, stirring frequently with a wooden spoon, until the polenta is very thick and pulls away from the sides of the saucepan, about 20 minutes. Stir in 3 tablespoons of the rosemary oil and ⅛ teaspoon of the pepper. Scrape the polenta into a medium bowl and chill until firm, about 30 minutes. Stir the remaining ¼ teaspoon salt and ⅛ teaspoon pepper into the remaining rosemary oil and set aside.

3. Heat the oven to 450°. Unmold the polenta onto a work surface and cut it into 8 wedges. Arrange the wedges of polenta on two baking sheets and top each one with a Cornish-hen half. Rub the hens with the reserved rosemary oil. Roast until the birds are golden and crisp on top and cooked through, about 20 minutes. With a wide metal spatula, lift the polenta and hens to a platter or individual plates.

MAKE IT AHEAD

You can make the polenta up to two days ahead. Keep it and the oil reserved for brushing the hens in the refrigerator. If the oil solidifies, simply let it come to room temperature. Once the polenta is set, you can also unmold and cut it in advance.

Wine Recommendation

A dry Italian white with character and acidity, such as an arneis or Gavi, would be excellent here, as would a red dolcetto.

47

Quail Wrapped in Prosciutto

SERVES 8

Instead of being trussed, each of these tiny birds is wrapped in a thin slice of prosciutto. In addition to making a delicious accompaniment, the ham keeps the lean birds moist during cooking.

16   quail

1¼   teaspoons salt

½   teaspoon fresh-ground black pepper

16   fresh sage leaves, or 1 teaspoon dried

16   thin slices prosciutto (about ½ pound)

1. Heat the oven to 450°. Season the quail inside and out with the salt and pepper. Set a sage leaf, if using, on top of each of the quail and then wrap each bird with a slice of the prosciutto. Or if using dried sage, rub the inside of each quail with a pinch of sage before wrapping it with the prosciutto.

2. Put the prosciutto-wrapped quail on two baking sheets and cook until just done, about 15 minutes. The meat should still be a bit pink.

MAKE IT AHEAD

Get the quail all ready to go hours before cooking, if you like. Refrigerate, covered, and bring to room temperature before cooking (about an hour should do it).

Wine Recommendation

The earthy, uncomplicated but delicate flavor of the quail allows a subtly aromatic, medium-bodied wine to show its stuff. Look for a pinot noir, which can add a note of smoky perfume.

48

Veal Chops with Mushrooms and Roasted Garlic

SERVES 8

Garlic cloves are roasted in olive oil until buttery soft. The garlic-flavored oil is then used to brown the mushrooms and the veal chops. It's easy to press the mellow garlic out of its skin with the side of a knife so that you can eat it with the chops.

40 cloves garlic (about 2 heads), unpeeled

½ cup olive oil

1 pound mushrooms, cut into quarters

1 teaspoon salt

8 veal chops (about 1 inch thick)

½ teaspoon fresh-ground black pepper

½ cup dry white wine

1 cup chicken stock or canned, low-sodium chicken broth

1. Heat the oven to 325°. In a small baking dish, combine the garlic cloves and oil. Cover with a lid or aluminum foil and roast the garlic in the oven until the cloves are soft, about 40 minutes. Remove the garlic with a slotted spoon and put in a medium bowl. Reserve the oil. Raise the oven temperature to 450°.

2. In a large frying pan, heat 2 tablespoons of the garlic oil over moderate heat. Add the mushrooms and ½ teaspoon of the salt and cook, stirring occasionally, until brown, about 8 minutes. Add to the garlic.

3. Season the veal with the remaining ½ teaspoon salt and ¼ teaspoon of the pepper. In the frying pan, heat 2 more tablespoons of the garlic oil over moderately high heat. Add four of the chops and brown well on both sides, about 5 minutes in all. Remove and put in a large roasting pan. Brown the remaining chops in the same way, adding oil if needed, and add to the roasting pan.

4. Pour the wine and stock into the frying pan and bring to a boil, scraping the bottom of the pan to dislodge any brown bits. Simmer 5 minutes. Add the mushrooms and garlic and simmer 5 minutes longer. Stir in the remaining ¼ teaspoon pepper.

5. Just before serving, cook the veal in the oven until just done (it should still be slightly pink in the center), about 12 minutes. Reheat the sauce if necessary. Serve the chops with the mushrooms, garlic and sauce spooned over them.

MAKE IT AHEAD

Roast the garlic a few days ahead, if you like. Leave it in the oil and store in the refrigerator. You can brown the mushrooms and veal chops and prepare the sauce several hours before serving. Put the chops in the roasting pan and keep them covered in the refrigerator. Either take them out an hour before cooking so that they return to room temperature or add a minute or two to the cooking time.

Wine Recommendation

Though these veal chops are cooked with a white wine, the earthy flavors will be wonderful with a smoky, perfumed pinot noir or a fine Beaujolais.

49

50

Roast Capon with Leeks, Apples and Pine Nuts

SERVES 8

Serving a large roasted bird is a practical way to entertain a group. In this recipe, juicy capon is matched with apples and leeks for a perfect autumn dinner. The brandy and herb butter that's spread under the skin keeps the breast moist and adds flavor.

¼ cup pine nuts

8 tablespoons butter, at room temperature

4 leeks, white and light-green parts only, split lengthwise, cut crosswise into slices and washed well

4 ribs celery, sliced

2 Granny Smith apples, peeled, cored and cut into ½-inch pieces

4 tablespoons applejack or Calvados

½ tablespoons fresh thyme leaves, or 1½ teaspoons dried

2 teaspoons salt

Fresh-ground black pepper

1 capon (about 8 pounds)

2 teaspoons cornstarch

1½ cups chicken stock or canned, low-sodium chicken broth

1. In a large frying pan, toast the pine nuts over moderately low heat, stirring frequently, until golden brown, about 4 minutes. Or toast in a 350° oven for 6 minutes. Put the pine nuts in a large bowl.

2. Melt 2 tablespoons of the butter in the frying pan over moderately low heat. Add the leeks and celery and cook, stirring occasionally, until soft, about 10 minutes. Add to the bowl.

3. In the same pan, melt 1 tablespoon of the butter over moderately high heat. Add the apples. Cook, stirring occasionally, until soft and light brown, about 5 minutes. Add to the bowl with 1½ tablespoons of the applejack, 1 tablespoon of the fresh thyme (or 1 teaspoon dried), 1 teaspoon of the salt and ¼ teaspoon pepper.

4. Put the remaining 5 tablespoons butter in a small bowl. Work in the remaining 2½ tablespoons applejack and ½ tablespoon fresh thyme (or ½ teaspoon dried), ¼ teaspoon of the salt and a pinch of pepper.

5. Heat the oven to 425°. Set the capon on a work surface. Stuff the bird with the leek-and-apple mixture. With your fingers, loosen the skin from the breast, being careful to avoid tearing. Still using your fingers, spread half of the flavored butter on the breast under the skin. Rub the remaining butter over the legs and thighs. Twist the wings behind the bird to hold the neck skin. Tie the legs together. Sprinkle the capon with ½ teaspoon of the salt and ¼ teaspoon pepper.

6. Put the capon on a rack in a roasting pan. Roast for 40 minutes. Baste with the pan juices and reduce the oven temperature to 350°. Continue roasting, basting every 30 minutes, until just done (170°), about 1½

51

hours longer. Transfer the bird to a carving board and leave in a warm spot for about 15 minutes.

7. In a small bowl, mix the cornstarch with 2 tablespoons of the stock. Pour off the fat from the roasting pan and set the pan over moderate heat. Add the remaining stock to the pan. Bring the stock to a boil, scraping the bottom of the pan to dislodge any brown bits. Simmer for 5 minutes. Stir the cornstarch mixture and add it to the pan. Simmer, stirring, until thickened, about 3 minutes longer. Add the remaining ¼ teaspoon salt and a pinch of pepper.

8. Remove the string from the bird. Spoon the stuffing into a bowl and carve the capon. Serve with the stuffing and sauce.

—*Katherine Alford*

52

MAKE IT AHEAD

Prepare the stuffing and flavored butter several days in advance, if that's most convenient, but don't stuff the capon until shortly before you put it in the oven. Roasted birds are best served relatively quickly, while the skin is still crisp and the meat moist. But since the capon must go into the oven about two-and-a-half hours before you plan to serve it, you'll have the work done well before your guests arrive.

Wine Recommendation

A flavorful, but not too heavy, wine such as a Beaujolais will work well with this hearty dish. If you're serving it after mid-November, a Beaujolais Nouveau would be fun for the full autumn-harvest effect.

Notes

Wasabi-Marinated Strip Steaks

SERVES 8

In Japanese restaurants wasabi is blended with water to make the hot, spicy paste served as a condiment with sushi. Here we've added it to our marinade to flavor the steaks somewhat more subtly. Powdered wasabi is sold in small tins or jars in many supermarkets and in Asian markets, and it keeps practically forever.

¼ cup rice-wine vinegar

2 tablespoons soy sauce

1 teaspoon Asian sesame oil

2 cloves garlic, minced

1½ teaspoons grated fresh ginger

1 tablespoon powdered wasabi

3 pounds strip steaks (about 3), about 1 inch thick

½ teaspoon salt

1. In a small bowl, combine the vinegar, soy sauce, oil, garlic and ginger. Add the wasabi and stir until it dissolves.

2. Put the steaks in a shallow glass baking dish or stainless-steel pan, add the marinade and turn to coat. Cover and refrigerate for at least 4 hours, turning occasionally.

3. Light the grill or heat the broiler. Remove the steaks from the marinade and sprinkle with the salt. Grill or broil the steaks for 4 minutes. Turn the meat and cook to your taste, about 3 minutes longer for medium-rare. Transfer the steaks to a carving board and leave to rest in a warm spot for about 10 minutes. Cut the steaks into thin diagonal slices and serve.

MAKE IT AHEAD

The steaks can marinate for up to eight hours, but don't leave them in the marinade for much longer than that or their texture will turn from tender-but-firm to mushy.

Wine Recommendation

The assertive flavors of the marinade call for a wine with good acidity and relatively simple character, such as a young Chianti or dolcetto from Italy.

53

Beef Tenderloin with Peppercorn and Mustard-Seed Crust

SERVES 8

A roasted beef tenderloin is always an impressive sight, but nothing could be simpler to prepare and serve. This one is coated with a wonderfully pungent mixture of crushed black peppercorns, coriander seeds and mustard seeds, and is served with an easy sour-cream sauce that features two kinds of mustard. We like this beef best hot or warm, but it's good at room temperature, too.

- **1** cup sour cream
- **1** tablespoon peppercorns
- **1** tablespoon coriander seeds
- **1** tablespoon mustard seeds
- **2** teaspoons salt
- **3** pounds beef tenderloin
- **1** teaspoon cooking oil
- **1** tablespoon Dijon mustard
- **1** tablespoon grainy mustard
- **¼** teaspoon fresh-ground black pepper

1. Line a strainer with a piece of cheesecloth, a coffee filter or a paper towel. Put the sour cream in the strainer and set the strainer over a bowl. Let the sour cream drain for at least 1 hour.

2. Heat the oven to 425°. Oil a roasting pan. Grind the peppercorns and the coriander and mustard seeds in a spice or coffee grinder or in a mortar with a pestle. They should have a coarse consistency. Add the salt.

3. Rub the beef with the oil and then with the spice mixture. Put the tenderloin in a roasting pan and cook until done to your taste, about 25 minutes for medium-rare (140°). Transfer the meat to a carving board and leave in a warm spot for about 10 minutes before slicing.

4. Meanwhile, transfer the sour cream to a bowl. Stir in both mustards and the pepper. Serve with the beef.

MAKE IT AHEAD

You can let the sour cream drain overnight in the refrigerator. Prepare the sauce up to a day in advance and refrigerate it; bring to room temperature before serving.

Wine Recommendation

Paging zinfandel—the true, tooth-coating red zinfandel, as nature intended it—or a similarly robust Rhône wine such as Gigondas.

54

Fresh Ham with Balsamic-Caramelized Onions

SERVES 8

Fresh ham, also called leg of pork, makes a delicious roast. It is most often sold with the bone in, so you may have to order boneless ham from your butcher. Without the bone, the meat cooks in less than two hours and carving is a breeze.

3½ to 4 pounds boneless fresh ham (leg of pork), rolled and tied

2 teaspoons salt

Fresh-ground black pepper

2 tablespoons butter

2 pounds onions (about 6), cut into thin slices

¼ cup balsamic vinegar

3 tablespoons water, more if needed

¾ cup chicken stock or canned, low-sodium chicken broth

1. Heat the oven to 425°. Sprinkle the ham with ½ teaspoon of the salt and ¼ teaspoon pepper. Set it on a rack in a roasting pan and roast in the oven for 20 minutes. Reduce the oven temperature to 325° and continue roasting the ham until it is cooked to medium-well (155°), about 1 hour and 20 minutes.

2. Meanwhile, in a large stainless-steel frying pan, melt the butter over low heat. Add the onions, 1 teaspoon of the salt and ¼ teaspoon pepper. Cover and cook, stirring occasionally, until the onions are very soft, about 20 minutes. Add the vinegar and water and cook, uncovered, stirring occasionally, until the onions are golden brown, about 15 minutes longer. If the onions begin to stick, add a few more tablespoons water. Remove from the heat and set aside.

3. Transfer the ham to a carving board and leave in a warm spot for about 15 minutes. Skim all of the fat from the roasting pan. Set the pan over moderately low heat and add the stock, the remaining ½ teaspoon salt and ⅛ teaspoon pepper. Bring to a simmer, scraping the bottom of the pan to dislodge any brown bits.

4. Reheat the onions. Cut the ham into thin slices and arrange on a platter. Moisten with the *jus* and serve with the onions.

MAKE IT AHEAD

The onions can be prepared early in the day. Reheat just before serving. Loosely covered with foil, the cooked ham will stay warm for at least thirty minutes.

Wine Recommendation

The straightforward flavors of this preparation will allow the exotic juiciness of pinot noir (including red French Burgundy) to shine.

55

Pork Tenderloin with Pomegranate Sauce

Prepare this dish with fresh pomegranates when they're in season, during autumn and early winter. Or you can buy pomegranate juice at Middle Eastern markets and some health-food stores any time of year.

1 orange

1 teaspoon grated lemon zest

½ teaspoon fennel seeds

½ teaspoon cumin seeds

½ teaspoon peppercorns

2 shallots, cut into thin slices

2 cloves garlic, chopped

2 tablespoons olive oil

3 pounds pork tenderloins

1¼ teaspoons salt

¼ teaspoon fresh-ground black pepper

4 tablespoons butter

1 small onion, chopped fine

1 cup pomegranate juice, from about 3 pomegranates

¼ cup dried currants

2 cups chicken stock or canned, low-sodium chicken broth

½ cup pomegranate seeds (optional)

1. Grate the zest from the orange and squeeze the juice. You should have about ½ cup of orange juice. In a large, shallow glass dish or stainless-steel pan, combine the orange zest and juice, the lemon zest, fennel seeds, cumin seeds, peppercorns, shallots, garlic and olive oil. Add the pork and turn to coat. Cover and leave to marinate at least 12 hours in the refrigerator.

2. Heat the oven to 450°. Remove the pork from the marinade and dry with paper towels. Season the pork with ½ teaspoon of the salt and ⅛ teaspoon of the pepper. In a large frying pan, heat 2 tablespoons of the butter over moderately high heat. Add the pork and brown well on all sides, about 5 minutes. Transfer to a roasting pan.

3. Add the onion to the frying pan and cook over moderately low heat, stirring occasionally, until very soft, about 8 minutes. Add the pomegranate juice and currants and bring to a boil, scraping the bottom of the pan to dislodge any brown bits. Add the stock, the remaining ¾ teaspoon salt and the remaining ⅛ teaspoon pepper. Bring back to a boil and cook until reduced to about 1¼ cups, about 15 minutes longer.

4. Just before serving, cook the pork tenderloins in the oven until done to medium, about 15 minutes. Transfer the pork to a carving board and leave to rest in a warm spot for about 10 minutes.

5. Meanwhile, cut the remaining 2 tablespoons butter into 6 pieces. Bring the sauce back to a simmer. Over the lowest possible heat, whisk in the butter in three batches, adding each batch when the previous one is incorporated. The butter should not melt completely but just soften to form a creamy sauce. Cut the pork

diagonally into 24 thick slices. Arrange 3 slices on each plate and spoon the sauce around the meat. Sprinkle with the pomegranate seeds and serve.

—*Stephen Kalt Spartina*

MAKE IT AHEAD

Begin marinating the pork a day ahead, if you like. Brown the meat and prepare the sauce a few hours in advance. Then just before serving, cook the pork and finish the sauce.

Wine Recommendation

Riesling and Gewürztraminer are both classic accompaniments to pork in German and Alsatian kitchens. And those wines, with a classic crisp acidity, balanced by a touch of sweetness, stand up beautifully to mildly sweet, sour and spicy sauces.

Information
Pink Pork Is Safe

For years Americans were advised to cook pork until well-done in order to prevent trichinosis, an illness caused by parasites in the meat. With today's higher meat standards, the illness is uncommon (on average, less than a hundred reported cases a year in the whole country). In any case, we now know that an internal temperature of 150° kills the parasites. At 150° even our currently available lean pork retains some juiciness. So cook your pork to medium, still ever so slightly pink, and enjoy the difference.

Tip
Juicing Pomegranates

We have to admit that extracting juice from pomegranates can be a messy business. Some people suggest first rolling the fruit on a hard surface to rupture all the pulp inside and then poking a hole in the skin and pouring the juice out. Sounds easy, but often the skin breaks prematurely, sending seeds hurtling all over you and your kitchen. The best method we've found is to cut the pomegranate in half and to squeeze it on a juicer or with a reamer, as you would an orange. Either way, the seeds scatter a bit. Put the pulp and leftover seeds in a sieve and press them with a ladle to get all the juice.

57

Side Dishes

Roasted Mediterranean Vegetables

SERVES 8

Roasting brings out the best in vegetables, caramelizing them to a sweet golden brown. An additional secret here is adding a little feta cheese and fresh herbs to the vegetables in the final stages of cooking.

- 1 large red onion, cut into 1-inch pieces
- 2 heads garlic, cloves separated and peeled
- 2 fennel bulbs, each cut into 8 wedges
- 2 red bell peppers, cut into 1½-inch squares
- 1 eggplant, cut into 1½-inch cubes
- 1½ pounds small new potatoes, cut into halves, or larger ones, cut into chunks
- ¾ pound baby carrots
- ½ pound green beans, cut into 1½-inch pieces
- ½ cup olive oil
- 2½ teaspoons salt
- ¼ teaspoon fresh-ground black pepper
- 3 tablespoons chopped mixed fresh herbs, such as marjoram, thyme and rosemary, or 1 tablespoon dried herbs
- ½ cup dry vermouth or dry white wine
- ¼ pound feta cheese, crumbled
- 3 tablespoons chopped fresh basil or flat-leaf parsley

1. Put one oven rack in the upper third of the oven and another in the lower third. Heat the oven to 500°.

2. In a large bowl, combine the vegetables and oil. Sprinkle the vegetables with the salt, pepper and dried herbs, if using, and mix well. Divide the vegetables between two large roasting pans and spread each batch in an even layer. Sprinkle with the vermouth.

3. Roast the vegetables in the oven for 15 minutes. Stir them and then switch the pans from one rack to the other. Roast another 15 minutes. Divide the cheese and the fresh herbs, if using, between the two pans and mix well. Rotate the pans again and continue roasting until the vegetables are well browned, 15 to 20 minutes longer. Serve topped with the basil or parsley.

—*Jim Flint*

Alternative

Red, Yellow and Purple Potatoes

If you want to make Roasted Mediterranean Vegetables, especially colorful, mix the potatoes. You can use half a pound of small red new potatoes, half a pound of Yukon Gold and half a pound of small purple new potatoes.

MAKE IT AHEAD

You can prepare all of the vegetables for cooking, except the potatoes, and toss them with the oil hours ahead. When ready to roast, cut the potatoes and add them to the rest of the vegetables. You can complete the roasted vegetables up to half an hour in advance and keep them in a 150° oven.

Recommendation
The Tough Herb

With Mediterranean-style grilling and roasting all the rage, it's easy to get carried away and start sprinkling rosemary everywhere. We love it, too; just make sure, though, that you chop both the fresh and the dried herb into fine bits. Even with lengthy cooking, spiky rosemary leaves remain hard and unpleasant to eat if left whole or in large pieces.

Recommendation
Keeping Fresh Herbs Green

Some fresh herbs, such as basil and oregano, turn brown soon after they are chopped. When using these herbs, it's best to chop them with a stainless- rather than carbon-steel knife and to do so just before adding them to the dish. Or you can chop the herbs in advance and immediately stir them into a little oil.

Notes

61

Spicy Green Beans with Garlic and Ginger

SERVES 8

This quick stir-fry can be made with broccoli, sugar snap peas or snow peas as well as with green beans.

- **2** pounds green beans
- **3** tablespoons cooking oil
- **2** cloves garlic, minced
- **1** teaspoon grated fresh ginger
- **1** scallion including green top, chopped
- **⅛ to ¼** teaspoon dried red-pepper flakes
- **½** teaspoon salt
- **2** tablespoons soy sauce
- **2** tablespoons chopped cilantro

1. In a large pot of boiling, salted water, cook the beans until tender, about 10 minutes. Drain, rinse with cold water and drain again thoroughly.

2. In a wok or large frying pan, heat the oil over moderately high heat. Add the garlic and cook, stirring, until fragrant, about 30 seconds. Add the ginger, scallion and red-pepper flakes and cook, stirring, about 15 seconds longer.

3. Raise the heat to high, add the beans and salt and cook, stirring constantly, until heated through, 1 to 2 minutes. Add the soy sauce and cilantro and cook, stirring frequently, until the soy sauce is reduced to a glaze, about 1 minute longer.

—*Stephanie Lyness*

MAKE IT AHEAD

You can boil the beans a day ahead and keep them wrapped in the refrigerator, but don't actually stir-fry until just before serving.

Tip

Great Ginger

Grate ginger on the small holes of a standard grater and discard the fibrous part of the root that stays in your hand. Grated ginger gives more flavor than minced.

Sautéed Greens with Peppers and Lime

SERVES 8

Two hearty greens, each with its own unique taste and texture, are sweetened with onion and bell pepper and spiked with hot pepper and lime. Three pounds of greens will seem like a lot, but they wilt to less than one-quarter of their raw volume. Don't omit a thorough washing, or the leaves may be gritty.

1½ pounds kale, stems removed, leaves washed well and cut into 1½-inch pieces

¼ cup cooking oil

1 onion, chopped

1 red bell pepper, cut into thin slices

1½ pounds Swiss chard, leaves and top 2 inches of stems washed well and cut into 1½-inch pieces

1¼ teaspoons salt

¼ teaspoon dried red-pepper flakes

2 tablespoons chopped cilantro

2 teaspoons lime juice

1. In a large pot of boiling, salted water, cook the kale until just tender, about 5 minutes. Drain.

2. Heat the oil in the same pot over moderate heat. Add the onion and bell pepper and cook, stirring occasionally, until the onion is golden brown, about 7 minutes. Stir in the kale. Add the Swiss chard, salt and red-pepper flakes. Cook, stirring occasionally, until the Swiss chard wilts, about 1 minute. Cover and cook, stirring occasionally, until all the greens are tender, about 10 minutes longer. Remove the pot from the heat and stir in the cilantro and lime juice.

—Stephanie Lyness

MAKE IT AHEAD

The greens can be made a few days ahead and reheated, but don't add the cilantro and lime juice until shortly before serving.

63

Corn Couscous

SERVES 8

Fresh corn and couscous are an uncommon match, but we find they complement each other perfectly. The corn gives sweetness and the couscous provides its buttery flavor and pleasant, soft graininess. Use frozen corn, if you like; here it's not a compromise. Serve this amazingly quick side dish with almost any meat or fish, as well as with Black-Pepper Seared Tuna, page 42.

3	cups fresh (cut from about 5 ears) or frozen corn kernels
1	quart water
2¾	teaspoons salt
2⅔	cups couscous
4	tablespoons butter, cut into pieces
¼	cup milk
⅛	teaspoon fresh-ground black pepper

1. In a food processor or blender, puree the corn kernels. In a large pot, combine the corn, water and salt and bring to a boil. Reduce the heat and simmer 1 minute.

2. Stir in the couscous and bring back to a simmer. Cover. Remove the pot from the heat and let stand for 5 minutes. Stir in the butter, milk and pepper. Serve warm or at room temperature.

MAKE IT AHEAD

You can puree the corn and measure out the remaining ingredients several hours ahead. That way it should take you only about fifteen minutes to cook the corn couscous before serving. You can also complete the dish up to eight hours ahead and keep it, tightly covered, in the refrigerator. Shortly before serving, heat the corn couscous, covered, over low heat or in a 325° oven for about twenty minutes, stirring occasionally. Don't stir too much; reheated couscous can get gummy. If you do make the dish in advance, add an extra one-quarter cup or so of milk to keep it moist. Or simply remove it from the refrigerator about an hour ahead and serve it at room temperature.

Orzo with Pesto and Lemon

SERVES 8

Pesto and lemon make a wonderful flavor combination that turns orzo into a perfect side dish for chicken or fish. It's good with meat, too. Homemade and ready-prepared pesto both work well, though you might use a bit more of the store-bought since the flavor isn't so intense as that of fresh.

1   pound orzo

1   cup Pesto alla Genovese

2   tablespoons lemon juice

4   teaspoons grated lemon zest (from about 2 lemons)

½   teaspoon salt

1. In a large pot of boiling, salted water, cook the orzo until just done, about 12 minutes. Drain.

2. In a large bowl, stir together the orzo, pesto, lemon juice, lemon zest and salt.

MAKE IT AHEAD

You can prepare the pesto for this dish and combine it with the lemon zest and salt several hours in advance. Press plastic wrap directly onto the pesto mixture so that no air gets to it. Then when you're ready to serve, you need only boil the pasta and toss with the pesto and lemon juice.

Sauce

Pesto alla Genovese

MAKES ABOUT 1 CUP

2   cloves garlic, chopped

1½   cups lightly packed fresh basil leaves

¾   teaspoon salt

½   cup olive oil

¼   cup pine nuts

½   cup grated Parmesan cheese

1   tablespoon butter, at room temperature

1. In a blender or food processor, mince the garlic and basil with the salt.

2. With the machine on, add the oil in a thin stream. Add the pine nuts, Parmesan and butter and whir just until the nuts are chopped.

MAKE IT AHEAD

Pesto will last in the refrigerator for about a week, or it can be frozen.

65

Acorn-Squash Rings

SERVES 8

These attractive slices of acorn squash are baked and served with the skin, which softens as it cooks and can be removed easily as the squash is eaten. It's shown here with **Roast Loin of Pork.**

3 acorn squash (about 4½ pounds), cut crosswise into ½-inch slices

6 tablespoons butter

½ teaspoon salt

¼ teaspoon cayenne

1. Heat the oven to 400°. Butter two large baking sheets. Using a small knife or a teaspoon, remove the seeds from the squash slices. Put the slices in a single layer on the baking sheets.

2. In a small pot, melt the butter with the salt and cayenne. Brush the squash with half of the butter mixture and bake until soft, 15 to 20 minutes. Using a wide metal spatula, turn the squash. Brush with the remaining butter mixture and bake until the squash is tender and golden brown, about 10 minutes longer.

—Rick Spinell
Spinell's Litchfield Food Company

MAKE IT AHEAD

You can bake the squash slices up to four hours ahead. Leave them on the baking sheets. Let cool and then cover them with plastic wrap. Fifteen minutes before serving, heat them in a 350° oven until hot through.

Tip

Easy Slicing

You'll find a serrated knife is the best utensil for cutting through the hard squash. The slices look prettiest as rings, but you can also cut the squash in half from stem to blossom end, put each half flat on the cutting surface and cut crosswise. This is easier than slicing the whole squash.

67

Sautéed Japanese Eggplant with Soy, Mirin and Sesame-Oil Sauce

SERVES 8

We love this unique and delicious way of cooking the small, narrow Japanese eggplant. The vegetable is sliced and fanned out, browned with a little oil and served topped with a simple Asian sauce. The dish is also good just drizzled with plain soy sauce.

½ cup soy sauce

½ cup mirin (sweet Japanese cooking wine)*

1 teaspoon Asian sesame oil

8 small Japanese eggplant (about 1¾ pounds in all), stems removed

¼ cup cooking oil

*Available at Asian markets

MAKE IT AHEAD

You can make the eggplant and sauce several hours in advance. Cook the eggplant and put them all on a baking sheet. Keep at room temperature. Fifteen minutes before serving, heat in a 350° oven for about ten minutes.

69

1. In a small bowl, combine the soy sauce, mirin and sesame oil.

2. Heat the oven to 200°. Beginning 1 inch from the top, cut each eggplant lengthwise into ¼-inch slices. Press the eggplant gently to fan out the slices. Brush the slices on both sides with the cooking oil.

3. In a large nonstick frying pan over moderate heat, cook three or four of the eggplant until browned on the bottom, about 6 minutes. Turn and cook until the eggplant are browned and tender, about 6 minutes longer. Put them on a large baking sheet and keep warm in the oven. Cook the remaining eggplant in the same way. Drizzle the eggplant with a little of the sauce and serve with the remaining sauce.

—Alvio Renzini

Cipollini in Marsala Glaze

SERVES 8

Simmering these small, flat, onion-like bulbs in Marsala and then cooking the liquid down to a rich, brown glaze brings out their delicious sweetness. Cipollini are increasingly available in specialty markets and are worth looking for.

- **4** tablespoons butter
- **2** pounds cipollini (about 24), peeled
- **1** teaspoon sugar
- **3** cloves
- **1** cup dry Marsala
- **½** teaspoon salt

1. In a large frying pan, melt the butter over moderate heat. Add the cipollini, sugar and cloves and cook, stirring occasionally, until the cipollini are browned, about 8 minutes. Add the Marsala and salt, reduce the heat and simmer, covered, for 15 minutes. Turn the cipollini over and cook, covered, until tender but not falling apart, about 10 minutes longer.

2. Uncover the pan and raise the heat to moderately high. Cook the cipollini and liquid, shaking the pan occasionally, until the liquid is reduced to a thick glaze, about 3 minutes. Discard the cloves and serve.

—*Erica De Mane*

MAKE IT AHEAD

You can make the cipollini a day ahead. Reheat gently on top of the stove.

71

Tip

Quick Peeling of Cipollini

Don't waste time peeling cipollini the way you would large onions, which would take forever. First blanch them in boiling water for about ten seconds. Drain, rinse with cold water and drain again. Cut off the root. The peel should slip off easily. You can also simply soak the cipollini in warm water for about half an hour to get much the same loosening effect.

Desserts

Warm Chocolate-Hazelnut Polenta Cakes with White-Chocolate Sauce

SERVES 8

Dark, rich and moist yet surprisingly light and airy, this Italian-inspired dessert is a lovely balance of textures and flavors that will delight even the most discriminating chocolate aficionados. We especially like the flavor of hazelnuts, but if you have trouble finding them or want to save the time it takes to roast them, you can use three tablespoons of almond butter, sold in jars in health-food stores, or even peanut butter in place of the hazelnuts. If you do use peanut butter, cut the sugar by one tablespoon.

¼ cup hazelnuts

5 tablespoons sugar

8 ounces semisweet chocolate, chopped

4 tablespoons unsalted butter

3 tablespoons coarse or medium cornmeal

½ cup milk

½ teaspoon vanilla extract

3 large eggs, at room temperature, separated

1 large egg white, at room temperature

White-Chocolate Sauce, next page

8 sprigs fresh mint (optional)

1. Heat the oven to 350°. Butter eight 5-ounce ramekins or 6-ounce custard cups. Put the hazelnuts on a baking sheet and bake in the oven until the skins crack and loosen and the nuts are golden brown, about 10 minutes. Wrap the hot hazelnuts in a kitchen towel and firmly rub them together to loosen most of the skin. Discard the skin. Puree the hot hazelnuts in a food processor with 1 tablespoon of the sugar until very smooth, about 3 minutes.

2. Melt the chocolate in a double boiler, stirring frequently, until smooth. Remove from the heat and stir in the hazelnut paste.

3. In a small saucepan, melt the butter over moderate heat. Add the cornmeal and cook, stirring, for 3 minutes. Add the milk and reduce the heat. Cook, stirring, until the polenta is thick, about 5 minutes. Stir in the vanilla. Add the hot polenta to the chocolate and stir until smooth. Cool slightly. Stir in the egg yolks.

4. Heat the oven to 375°. Bring water to a simmer for the water bath. In a large bowl, beat the egg whites until foamy. Continue beating the egg whites, adding the remaining 4 tablespoons sugar gradually, until they hold firm peaks when the beaters are lifted. Fold a third of the egg whites into the chocolate mixture to lighten it. Fold in the remaining whites until just combined. Do not overmix.

5. Divide the batter among the prepared ramekins. Put the ramekins in a roasting pan and pour in enough of the simmering water to reach about halfway up the sides of the ramekins. Carefully transfer the roasting pan to the lower third of the oven and bake until a knife inserted into the center

75

of one cake comes out clean, 16 to 18 minutes. To serve, unmold the warm cakes onto plates and pour the sauce around the edge. Top with the mint sprigs, if using, and serve at once.

—*Kevin Cauldwell*
San Domenico NY

MAKE IT AHEAD

The batter for these luscious little cakes can be made a day ahead. Put it in the ramekins, cover with plastic wrap and refrigerate. Add another four minutes to the baking time.

Accompaniment

White-Chocolate Sauce

MAKES ABOUT 2 CUPS

1½	cups heavy cream
6	ounces white chocolate, chopped
1½	teaspoons cognac or other brandy (optional)

1. In a medium saucepan, bring the cream to a boil over moderately high heat, stirring occasionally. Put the chocolate into a medium bowl. Pour the boiling cream over the chocolate and let sit for 5 minutes. Whisk until smooth.

2. Let the sauce cool and then stir in the cognac, if using. Chill for at least 30 minutes.

MAKE IT AHEAD

You can prepare the sauce ahead and keep it, refrigerated, for several days.

Tip

Melting Chocolate

Melt all chocolate using gentle heat to avoid scorching or lumping. Because the milk solids in white and milk chocolate are particularly sensitive to heat, they should be stirred almost constantly as they melt; dark chocolate need only be stirred frequently. The traditional way to melt chocolate gently is **in a double boiler**. Two other good methods are:

1. **In a microwave.** Put chopped chocolate in a microwave-safe container and microwave at medium until the chocolate turns shiny, about one-and-a-half to four minutes. Stir the chocolate until completely melted. Stir white and milk chocolate after one-and-a-half minutes. Do not overheat chocolate, especially white and milk chocolate, or it may become grainy.

2. **In the oven.** Heat the oven to 200°. Put chopped chocolate in a metal bowl. Stir frequently until shiny, about four minutes. Stir until smooth. We don't recommend this method for white or milk chocolate.

Tiramisu

Translated as "pick-me-up" from the Italian, tiramisu is hard to resist, with its espresso-infused ladyfinger layer topped with a light and creamy mascarpone mousse and covered with cocoa.

1½ cups hot espresso or very strong coffee

¾ cup sugar

2 7-ounce packages dried lady-fingers, preferably imported Italian savoiardi

6 large eggs, at room temperature, separated

1 pound mascarpone cheese

¼ cup unsweetened cocoa powder

1. Combine the espresso and ¼ cup of the sugar. Stir to dissolve the sugar and cool to room temperature. Line the bottom of a 9-by-13-inch baking dish with half of the ladyfingers, fitting them together tightly. Brush the ladyfingers with half of the espresso. Cover with a second layer of ladyfingers and brush with the remaining espresso.

2. In a medium bowl, beat together the egg yolks and 6 tablespoons of the sugar. Set the bowl over a medium saucepan filled with 1 inch of hot but not simmering water. Using a hand-held electric mixer or a whisk, beat the egg-yolk mixture for 5 minutes. Remove the bowl from the heat and beat the mixture until it is completely cool, about 7 minutes.

3. In a large bowl, whisk the mascar-pone just until smooth. Add the egg-yolk mixture and whisk until just combined.

4. In a medium bowl, beat the egg whites until foamy. Continue beating the egg whites, adding the remaining 2 tablespoons sugar gradually, until they hold firm peaks when the beaters are lifted. Fold a third of the whites into the mascarpone mixture to lighten it. Fold in the remaining whites.

5. Spread the mousse on the lady-fingers and smooth the top. Chill for at least 6 hours. Not more than 30 minutes before serving, sift the cocoa over the top. Spoon into bowls or onto dessert plates.

MAKE IT AHEAD

Tiramisu needs to chill several hours, and you can certainly make it a day ahead.

Tip

Savoiardi Substitute

If you can't find the dried Italian lady-fingers called *savoiardi*, the fresh su-permarket variety will do. They won't absorb so much espresso as the crisp ones; use three-quarters of a cup of coffee with two tablespoons sugar.

77

Chocolate-and-Toffee Gâteau with a Butter-Pecan Crust

SERVES 8

Deliciously decadent with layers of crisp butter pecan, sticky toffee and smooth chocolate, all topped with whipped cream and chocolate curls—this dessert's a real show-stopper. It's perfect for special occasions, and while it may look and taste complicated, it's surprisingly easy; each element in the recipe is quick to put together. We like bittersweet chocolate because it contrasts pleasantly with the sweetness of the toffee and the pecan crust, but semisweet is also a good choice.

1⅔ cups pecan pieces

¾ cup plus 6 tablespoons dark-brown sugar

9 tablespoons unsalted butter, 6 tablespoons melted and cooled

1 teaspoon vanilla extract

Pinch salt

3¾ cups heavy cream

12 ounces bittersweet or semisweet chocolate, 8 ounces chopped

1 tablespoon granulated sugar

1. Heat the oven to 350°. Butter the bottom of a 9-inch springform pan. Cover the bottom with a round of parchment paper and butter the paper.

2. In a food processor, process the pecans and 6 tablespoons of the brown sugar until coarsely ground. Add the melted butter, ½ teaspoon of the vanilla and the salt, and pulse just to mix. Press the nut mixture evenly in the bottom of the prepared pan and set it on a baking sheet. Bake the pecan crust in the middle of the oven until the edges are just beginning to brown, about 10 minutes. Cool on a rack.

3. In a small saucepan, bring the remaining ¾ cup brown sugar, the remaining 3 tablespoons butter and ¾ cup of the cream to a boil over moderately high heat, stirring frequently. Continue boiling, stirring occasionally, until the toffee almost reaches the thread stage, about 5 minutes. A candy thermometer should register 225°. Stir in the remaining ½ teaspoon vanilla. Transfer to a bowl and let cool or refrigerate for about 15 minutes to cool quickly. Spread the toffee over the pecan crust. Chill until firm, at least 30 minutes.

4. In a medium saucepan, bring 2 cups of the cream to a boil over moderately high heat, stirring occasionally. Put the chopped chocolate into a medium bowl and pour the boiling cream over the chocolate. Let sit for 5 minutes and then whisk until smooth. Chill in the freezer until very cold and somewhat thickened, 20 to 30 minutes. With an electric mixer on low speed, beat the chocolate cream until thick but still spreadable, about 1 minute. Do not overbeat or the chocolate will be grainy. Spread over the toffee layer. Cover with plastic wrap and chill for at least 2 hours.

5. In a medium bowl, beat the remaining 1 cup cream with the granulated sugar just until it holds firm peaks when the beaters are lifted. Spread the whipped cream over the chocolate.

6. Scrape a vegetable peeler along the remaining piece of chocolate to form small, delicate curls. Decorate the top of the cake with small mounds of the curls, using a mound to mark each slice. Chill the cake until ready to serve. Remove the sides of the spring-form pan. If necessary, smooth the sides of the cake.

MAKE IT AHEAD

You can make the cake through step three a day in advance. You can also get a head start by making some of the components even farther ahead. The chocolate cream will keep in the refrigerator for two days before beating, and it's actually better made well before assembling the dessert to ensure that it's as cold as possible. You can make the pecan crust two days ahead as well and keep it at room temperature. Several hours before serving, whip the cream, spread it on the cake and decorate with the chocolate curls.

Notes

79

Vanilla Semifreddo with Amaretti and Dark Chocolate

SERVES 8

A slice of this Italian-style dessert combines smooth and creamy frozen mousse with crunchy layers of crumbled amaretti cookies, chocolate bits and chopped almonds. Serve it in a pool of Chocolate Sauce.

¼ cup slivered almonds

8 amaretti cookies, crumbled

2 ounces semisweet chocolate, chopped

1 tablespoon cognac or other brandy

3 large eggs, separated

⅓ cup sugar

1 cup heavy cream

1 teaspoon vanilla extract

Chocolate Sauce, next page

1. In a food processor, chop the almonds. Add the cookies and chocolate and pulse until the mixture is finely chopped. Transfer the amaretti mixture to a medium bowl. Add the cognac and stir to mix.

2. Line a 9-by-5-inch loaf pan with plastic wrap, using enough so some hangs over the ends, and put it in the freezer. In a medium bowl, beat together the egg yolks and half the sugar. Set the bowl over a medium saucepan filled with 1 inch of hot, not simmering, water. Using a hand-held electric mixer or a whisk, beat the egg-yolk mixture for 5 minutes. Remove the bowl from the heat and beat the mixture until it is completely cool, about 7 minutes.

3. In a medium bowl, beat the cream and vanilla just until the cream holds firm peaks when the beaters are lifted.

In a large bowl, beat the egg whites until foamy. Continue beating the egg whites, adding the remaining sugar gradually, until they hold firm peaks when the beaters are lifted.

4. Fold the egg-yolk mixture, the cream and the egg whites together until just combined. Spoon a third of this cream mixture into the prepared pan and smooth the surface. Sprinkle with half of the amaretti mixture. Top with another third of the cream mixture. Sprinkle with the remaining amaretti mixture and top with the remaining cream mixture. Smooth the top. Cover with plastic wrap and freeze until hard, about 8 hours.

5. To serve, pull the semifreddo out of the pan by the plastic wrap. Peel off the plastic wrap. Cut the semifreddo into eight slices. Spoon some of the Chocolate Sauce onto each dessert plate, top the sauce with a slice of semifreddo and serve.

Information

Semifreddo

A luscious cold and creamy Italian dessert, semifreddo has a firm yet fluffy texture all it's own, different from that of ice cream or any other frozen dessert. The literal translation of *semifreddo* is "half frozen." It should start out thoroughly frozen. By the time you unmold, slice and serve it, the dessert will be just the right consistency.

MAKE IT AHEAD

The ideal do-ahead dessert, semifreddo can be made up to a week in advance.

Accompaniment

Chocolate Sauce

MAKES ABOUT 2 CUPS

The heat of the boiling cream melts the chocolate into a smooth sauce in minutes. Don't add the cognac until the sauce has cooled a bit, or the flavor of the brandy will not be strong enough.

1¾ cups heavy cream

4 ounces semisweet chocolate, chopped

1 teaspoon cognac or other brandy

1. In a medium saucepan, bring the cream to a boil over moderately high heat, stirring occasionally. Put the chocolate into a medium bowl and pour the boiling cream over the chocolate. Let sit for 5 minutes. Whisk until smooth.

2. Let the sauce cool somewhat and then stir in the cognac. Serve warm, room temperature or chilled.

MAKE IT AHEAD

You can make the sauce several days in advance. Keep it in the refrigerator.

Notes

82

Frozen Cappuccino Soufflé

SERVES 8

A frozen soufflé is a trompe-l'oeil dessert. A foil collar taped around the soufflé dish supports the creamy dessert as it freezes. When you remove the foil, the dessert looks like a high-rising baked soufflé. Individual soufflés (see box below) are shown here.

1¼ cups sugar

½ cup water

4 large eggs, at room temperature

4 large egg yolks, at room temperature

6 tablespoons coffee liqueur

3 cups heavy cream

2 teaspoons coarse-ground coffee beans

Unsweetened cocoa powder, for dusting

1. Cut a 30-inch-long piece of aluminum foil and fold it lengthwise in thirds. Wrap the foil around a 1½-quart soufflé dish to form a collar that extends at least 2 inches above the rim of the dish, and secure the foil with tape. Lightly brush the inside of the foil with flavorless cooking oil, such as safflower.

2. In a small, heavy saucepan, combine the sugar and water. Bring to a boil over moderately high heat and boil (brushing the inside of the saucepan occasionally with a pastry brush dipped in water, to dissolve any sugar crystals) until the syrup reaches the soft-ball stage, 5 to 8 minutes. A candy thermometer should register 238°.

3. Meanwhile, in a large bowl, using an electric mixer on medium speed, beat the eggs and egg yolks until pale yellow, about 10 minutes. Beat in the hot syrup in a thin stream. Add the liqueur and continue beating until the mixture is thick and completely cool, about 10 minutes.

4. In a large bowl, beat the cream until it holds firm peaks when the beaters are lifted. Fold the coffee beans and about a third of the cream into the egg mixture. Then fold in the remaining cream in two batches. Put the mixture into the prepared dish and smooth the top. Freeze until firm, 6 to 8 hours. Before serving, dust the top of the soufflé with cocoa. Remove the foil.

MAKE IT AHEAD

You can make the soufflé two or three days in advance. Once it's frozen, cover the top with plastic wrap to protect it.

Even Fancier

With just a little more work, you can make individual soufflés, using eight five-ounce ramekins. Everyone gets a miniature soufflé, and serving is easy.

83

Blueberry Crostata

SERVES 8

Anyone who likes blueberries will find this Italian-style tart irresistible. A delicate almond crust spread with cooked blueberries provides the base for plenty of fresh berries, baked just long enough to get them juicy. The method for making the delicious pastry is especially quick: Simply stir the dry ingredients into the butter and eggs. Serve each slice at room temperature with a dollop of whipped cream, or warm with a small scoop of lemon sorbet.

2 pints blueberries

5 tablespoons granulated sugar

6 tablespoons water

2 3-inch-long strips lemon zest

⅛ teaspoon cinnamon

2 tablespoons cornstarch

Almond Tart Shell, next page

¼ cup confectioners' sugar

whipped cream or 1 pint lemon sorbet

1. In a medium saucepan, combine 1 pint of the blueberries, the granulated sugar, 4 tablespoons of the water, the lemon zest and cinnamon. Bring to a boil over moderately high heat. Reduce the heat and simmer, partially covered, until the berries are very soft, about 10 minutes.

2. In a small bowl, stir the remaining 2 tablespoons water with the cornstarch until smooth. Add the cornstarch mixture to the pan and bring to a boil, stirring. Reduce the heat and simmer 1 minute, stirring. Strain into a bowl, pressing on the blueberries to get all the liquid. Let cool.

3. Heat the oven to 375°. Put the filling in the tart shell and spread it evenly. Spread the remaining pint of blueberries on top of the filling in an even layer. Sift the confectioners' sugar over the top of the tart. Bake until hot, about 20 minutes. Cool in the pan on a rack for 20 minutes. Serve the tart warm or at room temperature with the lemon sorbet or whipped cream.

MAKE IT AHEAD

You can make the cooked filling up to two days ahead. The dough for the tart shell can wait in the refrigerator for up to two days before you roll it out, and you can bake it a day before adding the fruit and baking for the final twenty minutes.

Almond Tart Shell

MAKES ONE 9-INCH TART SHELL

- ⅓ cup slivered almonds
- 1½ cups flour
- ¼ teaspoon salt
- 8½ tablespoons unsalted butter, at room temperature
- 6 tablespoons sugar
- 1 large egg, at room temperature
- 1 large egg yolk, room temperature

1. With a nut grater, or in a food processor or blender, grind the almonds to a powder. In a medium bowl, whisk together the almonds, flour and salt.

2. Using an electric mixer, cream the butter with the sugar until fluffy, about 5 minutes. Beat in the egg and egg yolk. Stir in the dry ingredients until well blended. Shape the dough into a flat disk and wrap tightly. Refrigerate until firm, at least 1 hour.

3. On a lightly floured work surface, roll the dough out to a ⅛-inch-thick round. Drape the dough into a 9-inch tart pan with a removable bottom and press the dough against the sides of the pan. Trim the pastry even with the rim of the pan. Refrigerate for 30 minutes.

4. Heat the oven to 375°. Prick the bottom of the shell every inch or so with a fork. Bake in the middle of the oven until golden brown, about 20 minutes. Cool and fill.

Notes

85

Mixed-Berry Cobbler

SERVES 8

Bursting with berries under a feathery-light topping, this refined cobbler celebrates the fruits of summer. Serve it warm topped with a scoop of vanilla ice cream or at room temperature accompanied by whipped cream.

½ cup brown sugar, more if the berries are tart

4 pints mixed berries, such as strawberries (quartered), blueberries, raspberries and blackberries

2 tablespoons kirsch or rum

¼ pound unsalted butter, at room temperature

¾ cup granulated sugar

1 large egg, at room temperature

1½ cups cake flour

1½ teaspoons baking soda

1 teaspoon cream of tartar

½ teaspoon salt

½ cup buttermilk

1 quart vanilla ice cream or whipped cream

1. Heat the oven to 375°. Butter two 9-inch glass pie plates and coat the bottom and sides with the brown sugar, leaving any excess on the bottom.

2. In a large bowl, combine the berries and kirsch and set aside to macerate.

3. Using an electric mixer, cream the butter with the granulated sugar until fluffy, about 5 minutes. Beat in the egg.

4. In a medium bowl, whisk the flour with the baking soda, cream of tartar and salt. Put the buttermilk in a small saucepan over low heat. Stir until just warm to the touch. Add the dry ingredients and the buttermilk to the butter mixture, alternating, in 3 batches, beginning with the dry ingredients and mixing until just combined.

5. Divide the berries between the two prepared dishes. Spoon the batter onto the fruit and spread in an even layer almost to the edge of the pie plates. Put the plates on a baking sheet and bake in the middle of the oven until the topping is well browned and the fruit is bubbling, about 30 minutes. Be sure the whole surface is a dark golden brown. Leave in the oven longer if necessary so the batter is thoroughly cooked. Remove to a rack to cool for 15 minutes. Serve warm or at room temperature, in wedges, with ice cream or whipped cream.

Even Fancier

For an especially attractive dessert, make the cobbler in individual dishes. Use eight shallow baking dishes, five inches in diameter, in place of the pie plates. Reduce the amount of berries to three-and-a-half pints so that the juice won't bubble over the edge. Spread the topping to approximately one inch away from the edges and bake at 400° for about twenty minutes.

Although no one would turn this down on the second day, the cobbler is best on the day it's baked. You can either assemble it a few hours ahead of time and put it in the oven about an hour before serving, which will allow time for it to cool down a little, or bake it several hours ahead and serve it at room temperature.

Recommendation

Using All-Purpose Flour Instead of Cake Flour

Because cake flour contains less gluten than all-purpose flour, it helps to produce a light and fine-textured cake. If you don't have cake flour, though, you can often just use slightly less all-purpose flour. For this recipe, remove one tablespoon from the one-and-a-half cups.

Recommendation

Baking with Room-Temperature Ingredients

When butter and eggs are at room temperature, they can swell to a greater volume than when they're stone-cold. Cake batter and cookie and biscuit dough blend more smoothly when all the ingredients, including flour and milk, are at the same temperature. When a recipe calls for butter at room temperature, take the butter out of the refrigerator at least one hour before you plan to use it. Cut it into half-inch slices, put it in a bowl and leave to warm up. Or if you haven't planned far enough in advance, use the microwave oven to take the chill off the butter. Cut the butter into pieces, put it in a microwave-proof bowl and microwave at low, stirring every thirty seconds, for two minutes. Eggs will take about one hour to come to room temperature. Don't pop them in the microwave for a quick warm-up—eggs microwaved in their shell will explode. Instead, put the eggs in a bowl of warm water, and they'll be ready in five minutes. Be sure the water is not too hot or the eggs will begin to cook.

87

88

Poached Pears in Cassis with Kir Sorbet and Lemon Pound Cake

SERVES 8

These pears get their intense flavor from crème de cassis, the French black-currant liqueur. The sorbet is based on a French aperitif called *kir*, a mixture of three parts dry white wine to one part crème de cassis.

3¼ cups water

3¼ cups dry white wine

¾ cup sugar

3 3-inch-long strips lemon zest

1 vanilla bean, or 1½ teaspoons vanilla extract

4 large ripe but firm pears, peeled, cut in half lengthwise and cored

2 cups crème de cassis

8 sprigs fresh mint (optional)

lemon pound cake

1. In a medium stainless-steel saucepan, combine the water, wine, sugar, lemon zest and vanilla bean, if using. Bring to a simmer over moderately high heat. Reduce the heat to low and simmer, partially covered, for 5 minutes. Add the vanilla extract, if using.

2. Add the pears and bring back to a simmer over moderately high heat. Reduce the heat and simmer, partially covered, just until the pears are tender when pierced, 8 to 10 minutes. Transfer the pears to a medium bowl. Reserve the poaching liquid. Pour the crème de cassis over the pears, let cool completely and then chill for at least 1 hour. Drain off 1 cup of the cassis and reserve.

3. Strain the poaching liquid. Pour 2 cups of it and the 1 cup reserved cassis into an ice-cream maker and freeze according to the manufacturer's instructions. Put a 1-quart container in the freezer to chill. Transfer the sorbet to the chilled container. Store in the freezer until hard enough to scoop, about 30 minutes.

4. Cut the pear halves into fan shapes by slicing them lengthwise into ¼-inch slices, leaving 1 inch attached at the top. Fan them out on plates. Pour the remaining cassis over the pears and put a sprig of mint, if using, at the top of each pear. Serve with the sorbet and a slice of pound cake.

MAKE IT AHEAD

All the elements of this dessert can be finished two days ahead. The pears improve on sitting as they absorb more of the cassis flavor and color. The sorbet maintains a perfect texture because of its high alcohol content.

89

Apple-Orange Crisp with Pecan Topping

SERVES 8

A luxurious version of an all-American dessert, this old favorite couldn't be simpler or more delicious. Vanilla ice cream would be the perfect accompaniment.

3 cups pecan halves or pieces

1⅔ cups dark-brown sugar

6 tablespoons granulated sugar

1½ cups flour

1 tablespoon cinnamon

1 tablespoon ground ginger

½ pound unsalted butter, at room temperature

2 teaspoons vanilla extract

8 pounds tart apples, such as Granny Smith (about 16), peeled, cored and cut into eighths

1 tablespoon grated orange zest

1. Heat the oven to 375°. Butter two 9-inch glass pie plates or baking dishes. In a food processor, chop the pecans fine. Transfer to a large bowl. In the food processor, put 1 cup of the brown sugar, the granulated sugar, flour, cinnamon, ginger, butter and vanilla. Pulse just until the mixture forms small crumbs. Add to the pecans and stir just until combined.

2. In a large bowl, combine the apples with the remaining ⅔ cup brown sugar and the orange zest. Put into the prepared pie plates. Sprinkle the crumb mixture over the top. Cover loosely with aluminum foil and bake in the middle of the oven for 35 minutes. Remove the foil and continue baking until the apples are tender and the topping has browned, about 20 minutes. Cool at least 15 minutes before serving. Serve in wedges, either warm or at room temperature.

MAKE IT AHEAD

You can make this dish hours ahead. Serve at room temperature or, if you prefer it warm, heat in a 250° oven for 15 minutes.

Alternative

Pear and Dried-Cherry Crisp

For a delicious alternative, use pears in place of the apples and toss one-half cup of dried cherries with the pear, brown-sugar and orange-zest mixture. The cherries add a festive holiday touch to the dish, and their slight tartness is a pleasant foil to the brown-sugar topping.

Espresso-and-Rum
Crème Caramel

SERVES 8

The French classic of smooth custard with its own built-in caramel sauce takes on a whole new dimension when flavored with espresso and rum.

2 cups plus 1 tablespoon sugar

1 cup water

1 quart milk

2 tablespoons plus 1 teaspoon instant espresso powder

6 large eggs

4 large egg yolks

¼ cup dark rum

1. Heat the oven to 350°. In a medium, heavy saucepan, combine 1½ cups of the sugar with the water. Bring the mixture to a boil over moderately high heat and boil (brushing the inside of the saucepan occasionally with a pastry brush dipped in water, to dissolve any sugar crystals) until the sugar turns a rich, tea-like brown. Immediately remove from the heat. Very carefully, pour this caramelized sugar into eight 11-ounce ramekins or custard cups. Rotate the ramekins if necessary to spread the caramel evenly over the bottom of each. Set aside.

2. Bring water to a simmer for the water bath. In a medium saucepan over moderately high heat, bring the milk, the remaining ½ cup plus 1 tablespoon sugar and the espresso powder almost to a simmer, stirring occasionally to dissolve the sugar and espresso powder.

3. In a large bowl, whisk together the eggs, egg yolks and rum until just combined. Pour the hot milk over the egg mixture, whisking. Strain the custard into a large measuring cup or pitcher and skim any foam from the surface.

4. Divide the custard among the prepared ramekins. Put them into a roasting pan. Pour enough of the simmering water into the roasting pan to reach about halfway up the sides of the ramekins. Carefully transfer the roasting pan to the lower third of the oven and bake until the custard is just set but still jiggles in the center when the ramekins are touched, about 30 minutes. Remove the ramekins from the water bath and let cool. Refrigerate until cold, at least 2 hours.

5. To serve, press around the edges of the custards to loosen them. Unmold onto serving plates.

MAKE IT AHEAD

Like many custards, crème caramel is every bit as good when made a day ahead. Keep the ramekins of custard in the refrigerator, covered with plastic wrap. If last-minute unmolding isn't convenient, you can unmold the custards onto dessert plates up to an hour in advance and keep them in the refrigerator.

91

92

Cold Orange Zabaglione with Raspberries

Light and refreshing, this zabaglione made with an orange-flavored dessert wine, such as Electra or Essencia, is an ideal complement to fresh raspberries. Of course you can always use the traditional sweet Marsala instead.

7 large egg yolks

¾ cup sugar

1 cup orange-flavored dessert wine, such as Electra or Essencia, or sweet Marsala

½ teaspoon vanilla extract

½ teaspoon grated lemon zest

1 cup heavy cream

1 pint raspberries

1. In a large bowl, beat together the yolks, sugar, wine, vanilla and zest. Set the bowl over a large saucepan filled with 1 inch of hot, not simmering, water. Using a hand-held electric mixer or a whisk, beat the egg-yolk mixture 5 minutes. Remove from the heat and beat until the mixture is completely cool and mounds when the beaters are lifted, about 7 minutes.

2. In a large bowl, beat the cream just until it holds firm peaks when the beaters are lifted. Fold in the egg mixture until just combined.

3. Divide the raspberries among 8 dessert goblets. Top with the zabaglione. Chill for at least 30 minutes.

MAKE IT AHEAD

The zabaglione can be made ahead and assembled with the fruit several hours before you plan to serve it. Eventually the emulsion separates, but it holds, remaining light and fluffy, for a surprisingly long time.

Tip

Folding Trick

Try the usual folding method with a different implement. Although most directions specify a rubber spatula for folding one ingredient into another, chefs often use a whisk. We find the many wires of a whisk fold faster and more thoroughly.

93

94

Green-Grape and Grappa Sorbet

MAKES ABOUT 1½ QUARTS

Because they're loaded with juice and have plenty of natural sweetness, green grapes make a delicious, pastel sorbet. Grappa, the Italian brandy made from the grape skins, seeds and stems left after winemaking, is added just before freezing to heighten the flavor and maintain the smoothness of the sorbet. Frosted grapes carry out the theme for an attractive and tasty finishing touch.

5 pounds seedless green grapes, stems removed

7 tablespoons super-fine sugar

3¾ teaspoons lemon juice

3 tablespoons grappa

Frosted Grapes, recipe follows (optional)

1. In a food processor, puree the grapes in batches. Strain into a large bowl and press the grape skins to get all the juice. Discard the skins. Add the sugar, lemon juice and grappa and stir until the sugar dissolves.

2. Pour the mixture into an ice-cream maker and freeze according to the manufacturer's instructions. Put a 2-quart container in the freezer to chill. Transfer the sorbet to the chilled container and store in the freezer until hard enough to scoop, about 30 minutes. Serve in chilled bowls or glasses and garnish with the frosted grapes, if using.

MAKE IT AHEAD

You can, of course, make any frozen dessert well ahead of time, but the sooner you serve sorbet after churning, the smoother it will be. After about twelve hours, even those with alcohol tend to get icy. If you make sorbet in advance, check it about

twenty minutes before serving. If it's very hard, let it sit at room temperature to soften slightly. While you can serve the frosted grapes after one hour, they're best made up to eight hours ahead and left to dry at room temperature. The sugary crust becomes even crisper—a pleasant contrast to the juicy interior.

95

Accompaniment

Frosted Grapes

MAKES GARNISH FOR 8

¾ pound seedless green or red grapes

2 egg whites, beaten to mix

½ cup granulated sugar, more if needed

1. Wash the grapes and let dry completely on paper towels. Cut small bunches, 5 to 10 grapes to a bunch.

2. With a pastry brush, coat the grapes with a thin layer of egg white. Sprinkle with the sugar. Let the grapes dry at room temperature for at least 1 hour.